Houseplants

Houseplants

A guide to the propagation and care of plants in the home

Lewis Parks

Edited by
Wendy Martensson

Cathay Books

Contents

First published in 1976 by Cathay Books,
59 Grosvenor Street, London W1

© 1976 Octopus Books Limited

ISBN 0 904644 16 2

Produced by Mandarin Publishers Limited,
22a Westlands Road, Quarry Bay, Hong Kong. Printed in Hong Kong.

Introduction

Growing plants indoors has gained in popularity over recent years. Not only is growing house plants a fascinating and varied hobby, but the results add charm to any household. There is nothing lovelier in a room than a flourishing foliage or flowering plant. It brings life and colour into the room softening its surroundings and making a setting seem brighter. And if the plants are the result of your own labour and love, their contribution to your home is even more important.

There are some people who think that they lack a 'green thumb' and that they are unlucky with house plants as a result. We hope to show in this book that much can be done to increase your fortune with indoor plants once you understand their requirements and are able to provide an environment in which they will be happy. There is a certain degree of trial and error in growing house plants just as there is in any form of gardening. A book can only give you general rules and tips on how to treat plants and what sort of growing conditions they prefer. The rest is learned from watching the plant and seeing how it reacts to the environment you provide and being able to adjust that environment when necessary either by increasing humidity or decreasing light or watering more or less frequently until you find just the right combination of conditions for each type of plant.

Of course some house plants are much easier to grow than others and it is a good idea for beginners to start with some of the simpler less fussy varieties so as not to be discouraged early on. As you gain confidence with these plants and come to understand how they react to different conditions, you may want to move on to some of the more exotic and difficult-to-grow plants. In the end, the only important thing is that you grow plants that you find attractive and that enhance your home. There is no point in growing difficult, showy plants if they are not your favourite types. Some of the loveliest foliage and flowers are provided by pot plants that are among the easiest to grow. So there is no need for specialist knowledge to fill your house with beautiful house plants.

The Dictionary of House Plants included in this book will introduce you to many varieties of plants suitable for growing indoors. This includes everything from the most common varieties to the most esoteric plants. Growing information is given about each one to give you a guide to the plant's likes and dislikes so you will be able to decide whether your home will provide a suitable environment for that type of plant.

The most vital thing about becoming an indoor gardener is that you enjoy the hobby. Growing cacti can be just as rewarding as growing foliage plants, and once you become a house plant enthusiast, there is no end to the reward you will receive for your efforts.

Choosing & Buying Plants

Before choosing and growing indoor plants, it is important to spend a little time considering the different types of plants that are available. House plants can be described as those plants that give a permanent display throughout the year. They are always green and do not have a resting period like many other plants. Some house plants are attractive because of the beautiful colour and form of their foliage, while others add to this loveliness by flowering. It might be usefully mentioned that although quite a number of them have common names, many are offered by florists under their somewhat incomprehensible botanical names. Do not, however, be put off by this, because they are quite easy to learn. In fact, it is often safer to use the Latin description because, in some instances, the common names are duplicated.

The second category of indoor plants that features nowadays quite prominently includes what are known as 'flowering pot plants', which are characterized by the fact that they have resting periods, during which, in most cases, they become quite uninteresting. Popular examples of this group are Indian azaleas, astilbe, calceolaria, chrysanthemums, cineraria, cyclamen, Cape heaths, hydrangeas and primulas.

Other very attractive plants grown indoors are cacti, succulents, ferns and palms, and plants from bulbs. In addition, there are the fascinating and often beautiful miniature and bonsai trees. These can very attractively supplement the decor of a room and for those inclined, raising and training them is an intriguing hobby.

When buying for indoors, the four most important considerations are (1) the conditions under which they are to grow, (2) the purpose to which they are to be put, (3) the experience of the owner and the amount of time that can be devoted to their proper upkeep and (4) the availability of sufficient space in which the plants may be stored when they are resting. There can be little doubt that many casualties among house plants have occurred because gift plants, given in all good faith, have not had these factors taken into account.

There are quite a number of things to be considered, such as the amount of light in the room, whether it is centrally or permanently heated, whether there are periods when it is cold, whether a plant is required for a permanently cold place, possibly a hall, or for a continuously sunny spot, and so on. Equally important is the purpose for which it is needed. A plant for a small table or an office desk must be compact and bushy, whereas a climber can be used to divide a room. Does a house plant that flowers or a foliage plant with coloured or variegated leaves serve the purpose best? It could be that, for some reason, possibly connected with the decor or the immediate view from the window of the room, colour changes are needed from season to season, in which case it is possible that bulbs and flowering pot plants are more appropriate. Lastly, there are several foliage plants that can easily spare some of their leaves. These might be invaluable to flower arrangers at a time when suitable foliage is scarce out of doors.

The choice of a house plant might be materially influenced by the circumstances of its owner. If you are a beginner, easy-to-grow plants are recommended until you have gained some knowledge. The more experienced could undoubtedly be more venturesome and grow the delicate and difficult plants, and perhaps ultimately turn a hand to propagation. Much must depend, even with the most expert, on the amount of time that can be devoted to the maintenance of house plants. A busy business person might easily find that he must limit his choice to the easy-to-grow and more hardy varieties. If there are periodical absences from home, it might be that cacti are the best choice. Providing they have plenty of sunshine and are not exposed to frost, they will exist quite happily at a temperature of 45-50°F (7-10°C) and with comparatively little water from late summer to spring.

There is one rather more unusual form of indoor plant which is mentioned at this point, because logically it does not fit anywhere else in this book. This is a miniature waterlily, growing in a large bowl, at least twelve inches in diameter. An excellent variety for this purpose is *Pygmaea helvola*, which is a very beautiful bright yellow. If it is planted in a box made from a piece of pretty, small-mesh plastic or metal netting, filled with good garden soil, which preferably contains a little clay and is not too sandy, it will flourish with very little attention, particularly if it is put on a sunny window-sill.

Finally, when buying always go to a reputable nurseryman or florist, if possible in your neighbourhood, so that there is little risk of damage when you transport plants home. A good grower will always harden off his plants, which have been raised in the warm, humid environment of his greenhouse, before he sells them to a flower shop or to a retail customer. An efficient florist will, in turn, look after the plants that have been delivered, they will be watered and kept out of draughts and they certainly will not be exposed to hot sunshine or cold winds out of doors.

It is always advisable to buy house plants, particularly the more delicate ones, in the summer, autumn or during a mild spell, so that they do not suffer any shock on being carried home on a cold, windy day. You should at any time make sure that any house plant is well wrapped to protect it on its homeward journey. You can be sure that a good florist or nurseryman will know exactly how to do this.

When making a choice, you should always pick out a plant with firm, brightly coloured foliage and without any pests, since these will not only damage this plant, but will also infest any that you have already at home. Particularly see that there is no damaged foliage, especially with those plants that depend upon their leaves for their beauty, such as *Ficus elastica* 'Decora', *Fatsia japonica* and *Monstera deliciosa*.

After it has been brought home, any house plant should be treated very kindly for the first week or so. It should be watered with luke-warm water, but only if necessary, and put into a warm place, out of draughts and full sun, to dry. Be careful you do not give it too much heat or water. After about a week it can be placed in its permanent quarters and treated normally.

Azaleas are often sold when they are in bloom. It is important to check that there are a lot of buds to come or the plant will finish flowering soon after you have brought it home. Once blooming is over, move the plant outdoors and either plant it in the garden or leave it in its pot to be brought back inside at the end of the summer months.

Growing Conditions

REGULATING GROWING CONDITIONS From the descriptions of the many different kinds of indoor plants it is evident that there are different aspects of cultivation and environment that have to be considered, if thriving plants are to be enjoyed. Good growing conditions are vitally important in making indoor plants happy.

Light : the fact is that human beings are able to keep more healthy, or at least appear to, in less light than plants need. As a result, most places in our homes are not light enough to suit the requirements of many indoor plants. Thus, keeping house plants at their best under such conditions is not an easy task. To start with, it is important to get rid of one assumption that might appear to be logical, but is completely erroneous, and that is that any shortcomings in this respect can be overcome by giving the plants long spells in direct sunshine. With a few exceptions, plants object to being exposed directly to the rays of the sun.

Dedicated enthusiasts to growing house plants can overcome this difficulty by installing cabinets, racks of shelves or planteriums, all illuminated with fluorescent strip-lighting burning for long hours during the day. Some people object to the altering strength of natural light during the day and create a completely independent environment for their house plants in a cellar, where the hours and intensity of light can be rigidly controlled.

Fortunately, the majority of us have house plants in our homes because they are pretty and add considerably to the interior decoration. There are, however, two important things that can be learned from these house plant enthusiasts and the research work of the plant scientists that provided them with their expert knowledge. These are that the majority of house plants must have good light

Below : Humidity in the atmosphere can be increased in several ways. Stand the plant in its original pot in a larger one filled with moist peat or else in a container which is made into a pebble tray. Alternatively give the plants a steam bath by placing the pot on a block of wood in a tray which you then fill with boiling water.

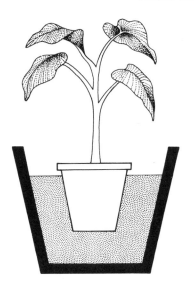

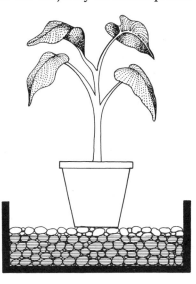

and that they appear to be as happy in artificial light as in sunlight. So important is the first point that emphasis is always given to those few plants that will tolerate poor lighting.

There are several things therefore that owners of house plants can do to meet the needs of their plants. The first is to always put them in the lightest place out of the sunshine in the room; secondly, move them as near the window as possible; and thirdly, keep the curtains and blinds fully open as long as possible during the day. If house plants have to be put into a dark corner, make sure that fluorescent lighting is provided to supplement the natural light. Spotlights have proved very effective for this purpose. It must be remembered that a grouping of house plants in a dark corner of a room has no value as a decorative feature. So light it up.

To achieve this end, it is best to use fluorescent lighting because ordinary light bulbs or reflector floods create too much heat, particularly in enclosed areas, when used in the numbers necessary to produce the required illumination. The latter varies from plant to plant and the higher the temperature, the more strength of, and exposure to, light is needed.

It has been found that for the best growth, plants should be given a source of light giving a balance of red and blue rays. This can be obtained by illuminating the area with one 40 watt, 4 foot 'daylight' fluorescent tube (for blue waves) and a similar sized 'warm white' (for red) placed approximately one yard from the plants. Effective alternatives are two similar, regular, soft white tubes or special fluorescent bulbs that give ultra-violet rays as well as light.

Warmth: the necessity of giving different types of plant varying degrees of warmth is very important to their well-being. Fortunately, in these days of central heating, the heat conditions in many houses is much more suitable for house plants than it was in former days. The big menace is fluctuations of temperature arising from fairly long periods early in the day when rooms are not heated much, then other periods when they might be overheated, followed by a rapid fall in the temperature during the night, perhaps even below freezing point. Such conditions are far more damaging for most plants than their being kept continuously in a steadily cool place. So in order to keep house plants healthy, put them in a position where the temperature is as uniform as possible. Always avoid, for example, standing them on the mantelpiece, where they might be roasted for part of the day, on the shelf over the radiator or, at night, behind the closed curtains on the window-sill, because it is likely to become intensely cold in so restricted an area. Ideally the aim of an indoor gardener is to maintain a continuous day temperature of 60-70°F (15-21°C) with a minimum of 45°F (7°C) or a little higher at night. If a plant is caught by the frost, it should be put in a position away from heat and sprayed with cold water. It might then return to normal.

Humidity: conditions in rooms are difficult for plants mainly because the atmosphere is very dry. The majority of house plants are evergreens from tropical countries and in the tropics you are only liable to find evergreens where the atmosphere is damp. In many parts of the tropics the atmosphere tends to be so wet that a number of plants have evolved, known as epiphytes, which can get all their nourishment from the atmosphere and have more or less dispensed with a root system. We do not want a moist atmosphere in our rooms, but it is possible to create a moist zone around the plants, by standing the pot or pots in some container, which

A Gloxinia is an impressive plant when in full bloom. Its large, bell-shaped, velvety flowers appear during the summer months in shades of white, red, purple or blue, some of them prettily marked and spotted. To keep the plants from year to year, gradually reduce watering once the flowers have died and store the dry tubers in a cool, frost-free place during the winter. When the shoots are an inch long, pot them singly into small pots of compost. Gloxinias can be raised from seeds sown in the spring or from leaf cuttings taken in the summer.

will either contain water or will contain some substance such as peat, which can be kept moist. You can put pebbles in a dish, nearly cover them with water and stand the pot on the pebbles, or you can get rather a deep bowl, plunge the pot in some moisture-retaining material, which can be peat, or sand or moss and keep this surround quite moist. Both these methods will ensure that water vapour will always be rising around the plant and the warmer it is the more vapour will rise, which is just what the plant likes. If the pot is stood on pebbles you should make certain that the base of the pot is clear of water.

Fresh air : a very important part of the life of an indoor plant is being given a breath in the fresh air. This can be done by opening the windows wide or standing them out in the open on a mild day

A large Philodendron Bipennifolium *makes an impressive pot plant in any home and is suited for life in an office as it requires little care. It is important for their health and appearance that you clean the large leaves. Shine them with a brand of wax made especially for this purpose which does not attract dust.*

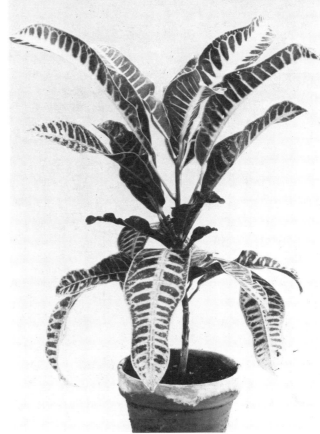

avoiding draughts. A little warm summer rain often does no harm; it helps to wash the foliage of the large-leaved plants. Opening the windows also helps to clear the air in the house of fumes and smoke which can be harmful to house plants.

Watering : the watering of house plants must be carried out very carefully. More plants are killed by overwatering than through any other single cause. If the soil is wet continuously, then air cannot circulate around the roots and so eventually the roots suffocate and rot and the plant dies. Often a beginner will leave a plant standing in a saucer of water. The roots start to rot and the leaves droop and this is misunderstood as a request for even *more* water. The rule is never allow a plant to stand in a saucer of water for more than half an hour. There are exceptions to this rule for example, *Cyperus diffusum* and *Helxine soleirolii* which enjoy 'getting their feet wet' and should be kept in saucers full of water, but such exceptions are few and far between.

The soil in a pot should never be allowed to become absolutely dry because some plants, *Ficus pumila* for example, might never recover from the drought. The soil in the pot should be kept just moist. There are several tests to see if a plant requires water. If the soil is dry, the pot will ring when it is tapped. If you tap the pot and the soil is wet, you will hear a dull thud. Also a wet pot is much heavier and the colour of the soil is darker than that of a pot which needs watering.

The problem is when and how much to water your plants to keep them happy. It is difficult to give a clear answer to this because it depends on the nature of the plant, the season of the year and the environment in which it lives. Plants with fleshy leaves such as cacti and succulents, do not require as much watering as plants with thinner leaves because they retain water in their tissues. On the other hand, plants with proportionately larger leaves require more frequent watering because they have a larger surface from which the plant breathes out water vapour.

There are two distinct periods in the life of the average plant, the season when it is growing and the season when it is resting. During the first, it needs plenty of watering and this should taper off as the dormant period approaches when the amount of water given is quite small.

Another important factor in deciding how much to water is the condition under which the house plant is living. When the temperature is high and the light is bright, its demand for water is greater. A plant kept in a cool place requires much less frequent watering. A plant requires more watering if it is kept in a well-drained pot. If it is in a clay pot, from which the evaporation rate is higher, it needs more watering than it would planted in a plastic pot. Plants in small pots and those which are becoming pot-bound need more watering. On the other hand, newly re-potted ones and those in large pots should be treated more cautiously. It is difficult, however, to give hard and fast rules. Generally it is better to underwater slightly rather than to water too much and to give plenty of water in spring and summer and little during the dormant winter months. It is advantageous to use water which has been allowed to warm to room temperature. Rainwater is ideal if this can be

The delicate fronds of the Aralia Elegantissima *add a lovely touch to a room and look especially effective placed against a solid-colour wall. Aralias grow quite large in the proper conditions but often shed the lower leaves as they grow. This plant is quite susceptible to scale insects so inspect the plant carefully from time to time to check for this pest.*

14

collected for the purpose, but tap water is not harmful.

Each watering must be thorough with a fairly long interval in between. A daily dribble is useless. Because of the possibility of chilling when the temperature falls at night, house plants should be watered in the morning during the winter. In summer, they should not be watered in direct sunlight as any water falling on them is likely to scorch the leaves.

In most cases, watering can be done either by plunging the pots in water up to half their depths and allowing them to stay there until the soil is fairly moist, but not waterlogged. After this the pots should be drained and put back in their place. The other alternative is watering from above, in which case it is important to be sure that there is a space of at least a half inch between the rim of the pot and the level of the soil. Use a watering can with a long, narrow spout that can be inserted between the leaves so that they do not get wet. Some plants such as cyclamen and saintpaulia can be seriously damaged by having their leaves and growing centres splashed; thus a sufficiently large pot is important.

This Gloxinia Hybrid is wildly speckled in the inside of the large flowers. Water these plants carefully so that no water falls on the large, hairy leaves. The safest thing to do is to water from below by standing it in a bowl of tepid water, and when the surface of the soil becomes moist, remove the pot and allow it to drain.

Bush Plants

Foliage house plants	Easy to grow	For average rooms in which the lighting is reasonable there is some sunshine and which are maintained heated for some hours daily during the winter	Unheated areas (halls, landings and staircases)	Especially suitable for centrally-heated rooms and other continuously warm rooms. (Care must be taken to see that the air surrounding the plants is humid.)*	Rooms without sun
Acorus gramineus 'Variegatus' (Grass)			●		●
Aglaonemas				●	●
Aralia (see *Dizygotheca*)					
Araucaria excelsa			●		
Aspidistra lurida		●	●	●	●
Aucuba japonica 'Variegata'			●		●
Begonia maculata				●	●
B. masoniana				●	●
B. rex				●	●
Bromeliads (Cryptanthus and Nidulariums)	●			●	
Calathea mackoyana				●	●
Cordyline (or *Dracaena terminalis*)		●		●	●
Cyperus diffusus (Grass)	●	●	●		●
Dieffenbachias				●	●
Dizygotheca (Aralia) elegantissima				●	
Dracaenas				●	●
D. sanderi				●	●
D. deremensis 'Bausei'				●	●
D. fragrans				●	●
Fatshedera lizei	●	●	●	●	●
Fatsia japonica	●	●	●		●
Ficus		●		●	
Fittonias				●	
Grevillea robusta	●	●	●		
Helxine soleirolii	●	●	●		●
Marantas	●			●	●
Monstera deliciosa 'Borsigiana'		●		●	●
Pandanus veitchii				●	
Peperomias		●		●	●
Philodendrons		●		●	●
Pileas		●		●	
Sansevieria trifasciata 'Laurentii'	●	●		●	●
Saxifraga sarmentosa (stolonifera)	●	●	●		●
Schefflera actinophylla		●	●		●
Setcreasea purpurea	●	●		●	
Tolmiea menziesii	●	●	●		●

* This is best done by placing them on wet pebble trays or packing them in wet peat.

Plants that flourish in full sun	Suitable for dark rooms and full shade	Small plants suitable for limited areas	Large plants suitable for offices and large spaces	Plants for flower arrangers	Plants that withstand fumes, e.g. gas, cooking, tobacco, etc.
		●		●	
	●				
	●			●	●
					●
			●	●	
				●	
		● *(Cryptantus)*		●	
			●		
				●	
			●	●	
			●		
			● *(Some)*		
	●				
			●		●
	● *(F. elastica 'Decora')*		● *(F. elastica 'Decora') (F. lyrata)*	●	●
	●	●			
			●		
	●	●			
	●	●			
	●		●		●
			●		
	●	●		●	
			● *(P. bipinnatifidum) (P. erubescens)*		●
		●			
●			●	●	●
				●	
			●		●
				●	
	●	●			

Climbers and Trailers

Foliage Plants	Easy to grow	For average rooms in which the light is reasonable, there is some sunshine, and which are maintained heated for some hours daily.	Unheated areas (halls, landings and staircases)	Especially suitable for centrally-heated rooms and other continuously warm rooms. (Care must be taken to see that the air surrounding the plants is humid.)*	Rooms without sun
Chlorophytum capense 'Variegatum'	●	●	●		●
Cissus antarctica	●	●	●		●
C. discolor	●	●	●		
Ficus pumila	●	●		●	●
Hederas	●	●	●		●
Philodendron melanochryson (andreanum)		●		●	●
P. scandens	●	●	●	●	●
Rhoïcissus rhomboidea	●	●		●	●
Scindapsus aureus	●	●		●	●
Syngonium podophyllum (nephthytis)				●	●
Tetrastigma voinierianum					●
Tradescantias	●	●		●	●
Zebrina pendula	●	●		●	●

Flowering Plants	Easy to grow	For average rooms... heated for some hours daily.	Unheated areas (halls, landings and staircases)	Especially suitable for centrally-heated rooms... humid.*	Rooms without sun
Campanula isophylla		●			
Cobaea scandens					
Columnea banksii					
Hoya bella			●		●
Jasminum polyanthum		●			
Aechmeas		●			
Anthurium scherzerianum				●	
Aphelandras				●	●
Beloperone guttata		●			
Billbergia nutans	●	●	●	●	
Callistemon citrinus		●	●		
Clivia miniata	●	●		●	●
Guzmanias				●	
Hoya carnosa		●	●	●	●
Impatiens petersiana	●	●			●
Saintpaulia ionantha		●		●	
Spathiphyllum wallisii				●	●
Vriesia splendens		●			

* This is best done by placing them on wet pebble trays or packing them in wet peat.

Plants that flourish in full sun	Suitable for dark rooms and full shade	Small plants suitable for limited areas	Large plants suitable for offices and large spaces	Plants for flower arrangers	Plants that withstand fumes, e.g. gas, cooking, tobacco, etc.
				●	
					●
					●
	●	●		●	●
		●		●	
					●
	●				●
				●	
					●
	●			●	●
				●	●
				●	●
				●	
●				●	
					●
			●		●
				●	
●				●	
					●
				●	
					●
●					●
					●
		●			
	●			●	
					●

General Care & Cultivation

Once you have provided growing conditions favourable for house plants, a great deal can be done in the way of care to maximize growth and flowering of plants indoors. Plants like to have attention paid to them and you will find that looking after your plants by keeping the leaves clean and shiny and keeping the plant in the right-sized pot free of pests will pay off in terms of how your plants flourish.

Cleaning and polishing leaves: indoor plants do not have their leaves washed regularly by the rain as do plants growing outdoors. Since the leaves play an important role in maintaining the health of the plant, it is necessary to see that their pores are free of dust and smoke grime and that a film does not form on the surfaces which will reduce the amount of light that reaches them. This is perhaps less of a problem nowadays with modern methods of heating. It is still necessary to keep a plant's foliage clean and it serves to enhance the plant's appearance as well.

Both the upper and lower surfaces of the leaves should be sponged with tepid water. If they are very dirty, soapy water can be used but it must be rinsed off thoroughly afterwards. Plants with finely cut or delicate leaves must be cleaned by thorough spraying. Plants with very large leaves can be wiped over with a clean damp rag or with cotton wool or even with a soft sponge.

Some people like to give the leaves a decorative shine, but olive oil, which achieves this end quite effectively, tends to attract dust, particularly in the pores where it is easily lodged. There is a proprietary wax emulsion that can be used without this effect to create a shine that lasts for months.

Feeding: pot plants need to be fed during the growing period of spring and summer but should not be fed during the dormant months or they will be undesirably forced. The exceptions to this rule of course are plants which flower in the winter and rest during the summer months in which case the feeding procedure is reversed.

Plants normally take in their food by means of the soil moisture and so it is easiest to apply the food in a liquid form. It is possible to buy plant food containing all the necessary elements sold in convenient ready-mixed liquid form. It is usually sold as a concentrate which is diluted with water and given to the plant as part of normal watering. Plants that grow rapidly need more food than slow growers. Climbers, for instance, need feeding once a week or so in the height of the growing season. On the other hand, the majority of cacti need no feeding at all. When a young plant is first potted up there should be enough plant food in the compost to last for a couple of months or so. Even when plants are re-potted, they seldom want feeding for two months because the tiny root hairs are sure to have been broken in the move and it takes some

This is an attractive selection of types of Primulas including the large flowered P. obconica *and the daintier* P. malacoides. *Primulas like plenty of water and light feeding when in flower, and it is comparatively easy to raise them from seed. A small azalea, a sanseviera and an ivy complete the grouping.*

Left : Stephanotis Floribunda *which produces lovely, highly perfumed flowers among its dark-green leaves, makes an attractive climbing plant especially when in bloom.*

Right : Give strong-growing climbers, especially those belonging to the grape-vine family plenty of room and encouragement to climb. Given support, they will soon cover a wall.

22

Above : The foliage plants which are growing together in this trough garden enjoy the same growing conditions. It is essential when planting this sort of dish garden to include plants of similar tastes.

Left : Campanula Isophylla *or Star of Bethlehem produces flowers in either white or light blue. This is a useful plant to use in a hanging basket or to trail decoratively over the front of a window box.*

time for the plant to adjust itself to its new conditions.

Probably the best time to feed plants is in the evening. This will give the roots a better chance of absorbing the plant food gradually. A plant only needs a little food so be sure to follow manufacturer's instructions and do not over-feed. An overdose will do a plant more harm than good.

Re-potting : this operation should be postponed as long as possible as most house plants flourish in what appears to be too small a pot. They do finally get pot-bound and have to be transferred to larger quarters. This is normally indicated by the slowing up of growth, rapid drying out of the soil and by roots growing through the drainage hole. It can be confirmed by knocking the plant out of its pot and examining the root ball. If it consists mainly of a matted mass of visible roots and little soil, then the plant needs re-potting.

The pot chosen for this purpose should be one size larger or two sizes at most if the plant is a quick growing one. In a clay pot, a layer of crocks should cover the drainage hole. This is followed by a thin layer of peat and another layer of potting compost. The plant is then removed from its old pot. The old crocks are taken away from the base of the root ball disturbing the roots as little as possible. Place the plant on top of the compost layer and fill the pot with more compost firming it down gently with slightly moist compost until the level of the base of the stem is reached. This should be about half an inch below the rim of the pot to allow room for watering. After tapping the pot down several times, water it and place it in a shady place for a week spraying it daily. After this time it can be turned to its usual quarters.

A group of plants consisting of Pellaea rotundifolia *at the back with, from the left, Mind Your Own Business, a peperomia, a croton, a Maidenhair fern and a Beloperone behind.*

A good potting compost for this purpose is a mixture of two parts commercial potting compost and one part garden peat.

Very large house plants are difficult to re-pot. This difficulty can be overcome by top dressing, which consists of removing the top one or two inches of soil from the pot in the spring without disturbing the roots of the plant and replacing it with a commercial potting compost mixed with a little commercial base fertilizer.

Indoor plants in trouble: like their outdoor counterparts, indoor plants are likely to be infested with pests and attacked by disease. The indoor gardener can do a lot to combat the effects of these menaces. If the plants are inspected regularly and the leaves are kept clean any pests can be picked off by hand before they get a

Right: This trough of foliage plants has been designed as a room divider in an office. A grouping of this sort is more attractive if it includes foliage of different sizes and shapes and variegated leaves. An arrangement like this can be sprayed with water to ensure enough humidity and to clean the leaves.

chance to multiply. If a disease is detected at this early stage, timely action can prevent it from spreading and becoming serious. No matter how much care is taken in providing plants with suitable growing conditions, they are still apt to become infested with pests.

Aphids or greenfly are common sap suckers which infest house plants. They cause the leaves and stem to become distorted and cover them with a sticky substance called honeydew. If the plant is infested it must be sprayed with a commercial pest killer. Red spider mites can be detected by the presence of a fine, whitish silken web on the undersides of the leaves where they live. The leaves acquire a metallic, greyish-bronze sheen, become brittle and fall off. Plants kept in a fairly moist atmosphere are usually not affected by red spider mites. If a plant is infested, spray with petroleum white oil emulsion.

White flies are sap suckers which cause the foliage to become mottled. Commercial plant spray is available to control these pests as well. If a plant is infected with scale insects, the stems and undersides of the leaves become covered with off-white scales interspersed with orange scales which are the young insects. The most effective way to combat this pest is to swab the infected areas with cotton wool soaked in methylated spirits. This same treatment is effective with mealy bugs which look like tufts of cotton and which feed on the sap of the plant stunting its growth.

The most common diseases which affect house plants are mildew and rot. Mildew covers leaves and stems with white powder and they become distorted. The affected parts should be sprayed and the whole plant sprayed with a commercial mildew repellent. Rot is usually caused by overwatering and water being allowed to remain

Below left : Chlorophytum Comosum *or Spider Plant needs little care to keep it happy. The mature plant sends out stalks which produce small white flowers and these become plantlets and hang gracefully at the ends of the stalks. This is a delightful plant to use in a hanging basket and benefits from having its leaves sprayed occasionally to remove dust.*

Below right : Hedera Helix Sagittifolia *produces five-lobed leaves which are roughly triangular in shape. The markings of the foliage make it an attractive climbing plant.*

28

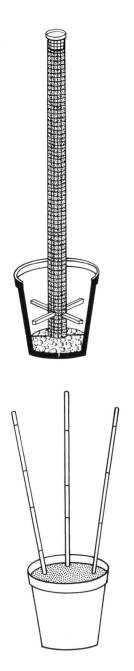

on leaves, stems and growing centres. The affected parts should be cut off if this is feasible.

Keeping plants tidy: like most living things, house plants can become untidy. Dead flowers and leaves should be removed regularly and any pruning to encourage growth or regulate shape should be carried out in the spring before the start of the growing season. The growing points of some leaves should be pinched out to encourage a bushier growth. This method is effective with plants like *Coleus* which tend to become stalks unless they are pinched.

If a plant needs supporting, you can use one thin bamboo cane or, depending on the plant, three or four placed around the circumference of the pot tied with twine or raffia. With feathery plants, it is possible to use twiggy sticks pushed into the pot when the plant is young so that the shoots grow in among them. Climbers that do not grow too rampantly are usually quite happy growing up a trellis-work stuck into the pot, or spiralling up a moss stick.

Encourage plants to grow by constructing a moss stick or totem pole. You can make it from a cylinder of plastic mesh filled with shredded moss and vermiculite mixed in equal proportions. If this is kept moist and is anchored in the soil of the pot, a climber enjoys sinking its aerial roots into it while it climbs. More simply train plants to climb up stakes or trellis networks inserted in the soil. Here an ivy plant is seen climbing a trellis.

Propagation

Gardeners will be familiar with the more common methods of propagation because indoor plants are multiplied in exactly the same way as those which grow in the open.

The raising of plants from seeds is a simple and easy method of propagation which most people try at one time or another. Seeds are the cheapest way of acquiring new plants for a collection except of course taking cuttings from plants already in the house. Remember that fresh seeds are the only kind worth using. Be sure to buy seeds from reliable dealers to avoid disappointment from old seeds which fail to germinate.

Layering is a particularly easy and satisfactory way of propagating some indoor plants particularly *Chlorophytum, Ficus pumila, F. radicans, Gynura sarmentosa* and *Saxifraga sarmentosa* which send out runners with tufts of leaves growing at their tips. If a slanting incision is made in the stem in the vicinity of this growth, the leaves removed and the growing point pegged down securely in potting compost in another pot, roots will usually form within about five weeks and the plantlet can be cut away from the parent plant.

Air layering is a useful process to use with plants like *Ficus elastica* 'Decora', *Cordyline, Dracaena, Dieffenbachia* and *Fatshedera* which lose their lower leaves as they mature. Cut a narrow ring in the bark at a point about twelve inches below the tip of the plant. Moisten with water and apply hormone rooting compound to it with a fine brush. Then cover it with a handful of sphagnum moss, which is bound into position with raffia and cover completely with a small sheet of polythene, which can be affixed to the stem with cellophane tape. When you can see roots through the polythene, cut the stem below the bundle of moss and pot the new plant. Cut down the remaining stem on the old plant to soil level. With watering and feeding new shoots will appear.

Plants such as *Acorus gramineus, Aspidistra lurida* and *Spathiphyllum wallisii* are propagated by division, a familiar gardening method of multiplying plants.

As with outdoor plants, there are three types of cuttings that are usually used for propagating indoor plants; stem, heel and leaf. They are all planted as deeply as possible in a rooting medium such as a commercial potting compost or a soil-less compost. The lower ends of the cutting can be moistened and dipped into a proprietary hormone rooting compound which facilitates the formation of roots but this is not essential.

Stem cuttings are taken by cutting a shoot just below a leaf joint that is about six inches from the tip with a sharp knife or razor blade. Remove all the buds and leaves from the lower half and plant the cutting to this depth. The ivies, *Rhoicissus rhomboidea, Cissus*

An Ananas Comosus *or Pineapple is a particularly novel plant to grow. Cut off a fleshy top with a rosette of healthy leaves during the spring. Remove the lower leaves to uncover about one inch of the bare stump. After it has dried out for a few days, plant it in moist sand and tie it to a stake for support.*

antarctica and some philodendrons are good subjects for this type of propagation. Cuttings of tradescantia, busy lizzie, coleus and ivies will form roots easily if just stood in a bottle of water.

Heel cuttings are usually taken from wooded plants. Tear a shoot off the older stem leaving a heel of bark. Reduce it to about six inches in length and remove all the buds and leaves from its lower half to which depth it should be planted.

Taking leaf cuttings is the method of propagating saintpaulias and begonias. An adult leaf is cut off at its point of origin, preferably in the summer or growing season, with a razor blade or sharp knife. The stalk is then inserted as deeply as possible in a rooting medium.

A particularly novel plant to grow from scratch is a pineapple. Either plant suckers or the leafy top of the fruit. With its silvery, long-toothed, curving foliage it makes a very beautiful house plant and it will often fruit two years after planting.

House plants can be grown from fruit seeds and pips such as the pips of citrus fruits which produce attractive little trees with decorative glossy, dark green leaves. The stones of apricots, avocados, dates and peaches can be made to produce very charming indoor plants but they are harder to grow than citrus pips.

Achimenes CUPID'S BOWER is a tuberous, summer-flowering plant. The funnel-shaped flowers, which can be various shades of pink, blue, lavender and white, grow from the axils of the leaves. The slender stalks require staking. It must be kept in a warm, light room, away from direct sunshine, and watered with moderation, keeping water off its flowers and foliage. It likes a moist atmosphere and does best if its pot is plunged in a second container filled with moist peat. Once it has finished flowering, it should be allowed to become dormant, its stems cut down and, if desired, the tubers removed for re-potting in spring. The tubers need a temperature of 65°F (18°C) to start them growing.

Acorus gramineus 'Variegatus' is a very attractive, easy-to-grow, grass-like plant, that grows upright to a height of about six inches. Its leaves are striped green and cream along their length. It needs light and a fairly cool position. *Acorus* will grow in water and is one of the few plants that needs 'wet feet'. It is a good plant for bottle and dish gardens.

Adiantum cuneatum MAIDENHAIR FERN There are several decorative varieties of this plant all of which require high humidity and a temperature of not less than 50°F (10°C). North, east and west windows are best, since the ferns are not so likely to dry out there as in a south facing window. It benefits by being given spells in the warm, moist atmosphere of a green-house or a steamy room. It has a very dainty appearance with each leaf being made up of numerous fan-shaped leaflets on thin stems. It is suitable for a bottle garden.

Aechmea URN PLANT These plants, which are members of the Bromeliad family, are characterized by the large strap-like leaves that form a vase-like rosette at their base. If kept in comparatively small pots, they do well in most rooms and are adaptable to cool or warm conditions provided they are given good light and kept relatively dry in the winter. Even in summer they should not be watered too heavily, but their 'vase' should be kept filled, if possible with rain-water. The varieties most frequently seen are *Aechmea fulgens*, with leaves olive-green on top and reddish purple underneath and which produces flowers and red berries that grow from a calyx; and *A. fasciata* (*A. rhodocyanea*), which has a rosette of leaves, striped in bands of grey and green, with small blue flowers growing from pink bracts. In both cases the flowers soon die, but the calyxes and bracts remain colourful for a long time. Neither plant is very tall, but can be more than two feet across and so needs plenty of space.

Aechmea fasciata see *Aechmea.*

Achmea fulgens see *Aechmea.*

Aechmea rhodocyanea see *Aechmea.*

Adiantum cuneatum

Aechmea Rhodocyanea *is a dramatic showpiece when in bloom. The flower, which is at the end of a long stalk growing from the centre of the plant's 'vase', lasts for about two weeks before beginning to fade. The plant provides a decorative accent in any room even when it is not in bloom.*

Anthurium scherzerianum

Anthurium

Aeschyanthus speciosus LIPSTICK VINE is a beautiful plant for indoor decoration. It has long stems bearing lovely fleshy, deep-green, narrow leaves and clusters of orange, tubular, fragrant flowers at their extremities. It is either grown in hanging baskets or as a climber on supports in pots.

It should be planted in a rich mixture of sifted leaf-mould and a little sphagnum moss and should be re-potted each year. It likes good drainage and high humidity. It should be well watered in the summer and kept reasonably dry during winter at a temperature of about 50°F (10°C). It should not be allowed to flower.

AFRICAN VIOLET see *Saintpaulia ionantha*.

Aglaonema commutatum CHINESE EVERGREEN This is not an easy plant to grow. To be successful, it should be maintained at a temperature of 60-70°F (15-21°C), with no winter fluctuations. It likes shade and moisture. It should be watered well and given liquid manure during summer, with only a little watering during the winter. It appreciates being sprayed with clean water in hot and dry weather. With its nine-inch long, dark-green leaves that are blotched white, it is an attractive plant. So is its compact cultivar 'Silver Queen' which has silvery-grey leaves.

ALUMINIUM PLANT see *Pilea cadierei*.

Amaryllis has spectacular flowers and is easy to grow in the house. Plant the bulb in potting compost in mid-October so that it is halfway out of the soil. Give it bottom warmth by placing it on a warm shelf, say, over a radiator. When buds form, transfer to a sunny window-sill, watering sparingly at first and then freely, *always from the top*. To keep for the next season, put it in a cool place after flowering, watering until growth stops and then almost cease watering. Next spring, top-dress with fresh soil and increase watering steadily.

Ananus comosus 'Variegatus' VARIEGATED PINEAPPLE is a member of the Bromeliad family. This is a very beautiful house plant with long serrated pointed leaves, with lengthwise stripes, green in the centre flanked by yellow, tinged red towards the edges.

Anthurium scherzerianum FLAMINGO PLANT, PAINTER'S PALETTE is an impressive house plant. It is a difficult one to grow because it needs to be kept in a well-heated room, in which there are no temperature changes. A constant temperature of 60°F (15°C) is ideal. It needs to be planted in a well-drained pot, surrounded by moist peat so that the atmosphere is moist and to be given plenty of water. In the winter the peat should be reduced, but the plant

Above left : Here a variety of bromeliads, Aechmea Fasciata all display their dramatic blooms. Often plants of this sort are in bloom when they are bought and it may take a long time before they can be encouraged to bloom again while they adjust to new conditions.

Above right : This attractive foliage plant, Aglaonema Treubii is related to the Chinese Evergreen. Its leaves will look their best if the plant is grown in a well-lit position.

must not be allowed to dry out. Frequent spraying with tepid water is an advantage. It should be placed in a well-lit place. *A. scherzerianum* is a very colourful plant and is the best flowering variety. It has long, slender, shiny, lanceolate leaves, but its crowning glory is its wonderful wax-like, flamboyant, scarlet flowers, which grow on tall red stems and are composed of a spathe about two to three inches long and the same width, and a spirally-twisted orange-red spadix. The combination of these gives the plant an unusual, but most attractive, appearance. Illustrated in colour on page 51.

Aphelandra squarrosa 'Louisae' ZEBRA PLANT is a rather difficult, but very showy plant, which is well worth growing. It has been found that younger plants are more adaptable to house conditions than larger ones. It needs to be in a well-lit, but not sunlit, spot in which there is always moist and warm air. Its winter temperature should never be lower than 55°F (13°C). Its soil should be kept constantly moist in the summer, but not soggy, and on the dry side in the winter. Spraying the foliage is very advantageous.

Aralia elegantissima

It is a beautiful plant with ten-inch long, pointed, very dark-green leaves, of which the veins are boldly delineated in pale cream. Its beauty is further enhanced by its large yellow flowers, which should be removed after they fade. Very beautiful varieties are 'Brockfield' and 'Silver Beauty'.

Aralia see *Fatsia japonica*.

Aralia elegantissima FINGER ARALIA Its unusual finger-like, long narrow leaves, not more than half an inch wide, make this a most graceful house plant. They are deeply serrated and spread out in a flat plane at the end of its dark-green, mottled stalks. The young foliage is reddish brown, becoming almost black with age.

It is not easy to grow and requires warmth (60°F, 15°C) and moisture, particularly during winter, and good light. Draughts and fluctuations in temperature must be avoided. It should not be over-watered. If deprived of light and humidity, it will lose its leaves, particularly the lower ones, and there is no way to restore this loss except to cut back the plant and wait for new growth to appear. Also known as *Dizygotheca elegantissima*.

Below left : Aphelandra Squarrosa *Brockfield is one variety of Zebra Plant, and is often sold when in bloom. Do not be discouraged when the flowers fade, because although this is not an easy plant to grow, with patience it will flower again.*

Below right : These bromeliads, Aechmea Orlandiana *are growing imbedded in a piece of driftwood. If bromeliads are planted in this way as small plants they will often flower successfully when the plants mature.*

Araucaria excelsa

Araucaria excelsa NORFOLK ISLAND PINE This wonderful pot plant is related to the monkey-puzzle tree and grows to a height of 100-150 feet in its natural habitat. Kept in a small pot it becomes dwarfed. It has very beautiful layers of emerald-green needles, which makes it an excellent permanent Christmas tree. In a cool, light or shady room, it will grow slowly for a long time if it is kept moist. Should the needles begin to fall, the pot should be stood on a pebble tray. Illustrated in colour on page 54.

ARTILLERY PLANT see *Pilea muscosa*.

ASPARAGUS FERN Although these are not true ferns, but members of the Lily family, they are regarded as ferns by most people. They are delicate plants and have feathery foliage; if lopped they can be kept reasonably low-growing. There is, however, a dwarf variety, *A. plumosus* 'Compactus' which is excellent for small pots. Asparagus fern is treasured by florists and flower arrangers alike because it makes such a beautiful foil to almost any flowers.

Asparagus plumosus see ASPARAGUS FERN.

Asparagus plumosus 'Compactus' see ASPARAGUS FERN.

Asparagus sprengeri see ASPARAGUS FERN.

Aspidistra elatior see *Aspidistra lurida*.

Aspidistra lurida CAST IRON PLANT This plant was a favourite during the nineteenth century and the earlier decades of the twentieth, but although much cherished by flower arrangers, particularly in its variegated form, it is something of a rarity nowadays, because, being a slow grower, it is costly to raise. Tough, as its first popular name suggests, it tolerates shade, dust, dry air and soil, but dislikes bright sunshine. What it likes ideally is to be given a reasonable supply of moisture, medium humidity and fair warmth. It loves a day out in warm, summer rain and regular washing with

Below left : Aphelandra Chamissioniana *is a more showy variety of* Aphelandra.

Below right : This Azalea Indica *is pruned into a particularly delightful shape. Grown indoors azaleas make pleasant and decorative shrubs which produce long-lasting abundant flowers.*

The delicate foliage of the Asparagus Plumosus Nanus *is much prized. Although this fern is a sensitive plant to grow, it can be grown successfully if kept in a humid, not too warm atmosphere*

tepid water. Illustrated in colour on page 51.

Astilbe SPIRAEA These plants bear large plumes of white, pink or red flowers, which rise above their light-green foliage. They are not difficult to grow if they are placed in a room where there is plenty of sun and are watered freely when coming into flower. After flowering, the more hardy varieties, such as *Astilbe rosea*, and the varieties 'Peach Blossom' and 'Queen Alexandra' can be transferred to the garden and dug up and re-potted in early spring. The more tender *A. japonica* should be plunged into the soil and brought indoors again before the frost comes.

AUSTRALIAN WATTLE see *Grevillea robusta*.

Azalea indica The many varieties of Indian azaleas are the most valuable of all flowering house plants, because they are laden with red, pink or white blooms during the winter months. Many people find them difficult to grow in the house but success can be attained if they are kept in a well-lit, airy spot, out of direct sunlight. They need to be kept fairly warm and out of draughts. It is advantageous to surround the pot with damp peat. They require to be kept continuously moist and are best watered by allowing the pot to stand up to the rim in water. It is also beneficial to feed them regularly during the blooming season. If the dead flowers are removed without any delay, the flowering season is lengthened. *A. indica* can be preserved by plunging the pot into the soil out of doors in May, after the danger of frost has passed. Here it can remain until autumn although check that it does not dry out completely. When it is necessary to re-pot, a good medium is lime-free, sterilized soil containing a proportion of pine-needle peat. Illustrated in colour on page 44.

Aspidistra lurida

Begonia rex

BABY'S TEARS see *Helxine soleirolii.*
BAMBOO PALM see *Chamaedorea erumpens.*
BARBADOS HEATHER see *Cuphea hyssopifolia.*
BAYONET PLANT see *Sansevieria trifasciata* 'Laurentii'.
BAY TREE see *Lauris nobilis.*

Begonias These popular plants like a well-lit place, far away from fumes. They are best when their pot is surrounded by damp peat. They need to be watered well in the growing season and kept comparatively dry when they are resting. The leaves should on no account be wetted. In winter a temperature of 50-55°F (10-13°C) should always be maintained. There are climbing and bushy types.

The most recommended climbing species is *Begonia glaucophylla,* which has shiny, pointed, greyish-green leaves, which make a very lovely foil for its brick-red flowers in pendulous clusters, which appear in spring and summer. It is also an excellent plant for hanging baskets. It does not like hot rooms. *B. glabra* is another suitable climbing begonia; it has small white flowers.

Among the more bushy types of begonias that flower well are *B. maculata,* which has very decorative, large, medium-green leaves, that are brightly spotted with silver. It produces pendulous bunches of bright-pink flowers for a long period at almost any time of the year.

B. emanicata is a winter-blooming begonia which has erect flowering stems that bear small rose-pink flowers. The Christmas begonia (Gloire de Lorraine Begonia), *B. cheimantha* which gives a dense mass of bright-red or pink blooms in the winter, is usually discarded after flowering, but given a warm, light, humid position, with moderate watering it can be made more permanent. The small fibrous-rooted begonia, *B. semperflorens* and its many varieties make quite excellent house plants, particularly if two cultivars of different colour are planted in the same small pot. They like the sun.

Probably the most decorative of all begonias, which is grown for the beauty of its foliage, is the bushy *B. rex.* The colour of its large, approximately triangular leaves covers a wide range from silver to dark green and pink to the darkest purple. The patterns on the leaves are almost indescribable and are composed of dots, stripes

Above left : There are so many varieties of begonia that this is one of the most popular of all house-plants. They are easy to grow and can be depended on to produce lovely flowers during much of the year.

Above right : This Begonia Masoniana or Iron Cross Begonia gets its common name from the striking markings on the leaves and produces fairly insignificant pink blooms at the ends of long stalks.

38

The Beloperone Guttata *is a free-flowering attractive shrub whose distinctively shaped flowers have earned it the common name of Shrimp Plant. It can be easily reproduced from cuttings in the spring.*

and splashes of numerous contrasting colours with bands on their edges and the path of their veins. Superimposed on all this glamour is an exquisite metallic sheen. Another low-growing, bushy, foliage begonia is *B. masoniana*, which, because of the purplish-brown Iron Cross marked on the medium-green background of each of its leaves is commonly known as the 'Iron Cross Begonia'. It grows into an extremely distinctive plant.

These species are indeed superb and put up the most glorious display when planted either as specimens or in groupings, either in dishes or bottle gardens.

Begonia cheimantha see *Begonias.*
Begonia glabra see *Begonias.*
Begonia glaucophylla see *Begonias.*
Begonia maculata see *Begonias.*
Begonia manicata see *Begonias.*
Begonia masoniana see *Begonias.*
Begonia rex see *Begonias.*

Beloperone guttata

Begonia semperflorens see *Begonias*.

Beloperone guttata SHRIMP PLANT The shrimp-coloured bracts and white flowers are what give this easy-to-grow plant its common name. It does well in a sunny window where it will bloom most of the time. It needs plenty of water and regular feeding in spring and summer with occasional spraying when the weather is hot. It should be kept cool and dryish in winter. Prune the plant in the spring to keep its busy shape. Illustrated in colour on page 48.

Billbergia PITCHER PLANT These bromeliads are easy and rewarding to grow. They tolerate cool winter conditions and dry air. They should be put in a well-lighted spot as light and warmth encourages flowering. Do not overwater but give liquid food while they are growing.

Billbergia nutans QUEEN'S TEARS This plant is almost hardy. It has narrow, twelve-inch long, evergreen leaves. It produces tall flowering stalks, which are surmounted by unusual, but picturesque nodding, transient, yellowish-green, violet-blue-bordered flowers, that are accompanied by a pink bract, which persists five or six days after the blooms fade.

B. windii This variety has boat-shaped, rosy-red bracts and flowers that are suffused with reddish-purple and greenish-yellow.

BIRD'S NEST BROMELIAD see *Nidularium fulgens*.

BLACK-EYED SUSAN see *Thunbergia alata*.

BOAT LILY see *Rhoeo discolor*.

BOSTON FERN see *Nephrolepsis exaltata bostoniensis*.

BOTTLE BRUSH PLANT see *Callistemon citrinus*.

BRAKE FERN see *Pteris cretica*.

BUSY LIZZIE see *Impatiens petersiana*.

The Dictionary of Indoor Plants is continued on page 57.

Above left : This variety of Begonia, B. Manicata produces lovely clustering blooms which give the plant a delicate lacy look. It is much prized for profusion.

Above right : The Bilbergia Windii produces elegant flowers on long stalks, and has rosettes of long, narrow leaves. It should be kept out of direct sunlight.

Right : The dazzling foliage of this Caladium Hybrid makes it an excellent choice for a room which is lacking in colour. Take care not to overwater Caladiums as the leaves rot fairly easily and they are difficult to restart if this happens.

Passiflora *John Innes*
*produces a vibrant and
dramatic flower un-
rivalled for its intensity
of colour. Support this
climbing plant on stakes
around which it wraps
its creeping tendrils.*

*Right : Although
hydrangeas are more
commonly grown out-
doors, they make charm-
ing and decorative house
plants and you should
move them to the garden
when they have finished
flowering. This variety
is* Hydrangea Hortensis.

Above : Rhododendron simsii, *better known as azaleas, provide profuse blooms. It is essential that you never allow the root ball to dry out.*

Below : Primula obconica *is a winter blooming primrose. When choosing a plant be sure that there are plenty of buds and that the leaves are a fresh green with firm and upstanding stems.*

Right : Saintpaulia ionantha *'Diana Blue' is an excellent strain of African Violet. It grows well, given a good light, clean air, humidity and feeding when in flower.*

Far left : Stephanotis floribunda *has extremely beautiful waxen flowers with a rich scent which can prove overpowering in an enclosed space. They grow in clusters or bunches along the length of the stems which may need supporting. Spray the plant occasionally to maintain the humidity.*

Left : Jasminum mesnyi *is a dual-purpose plant which is happy growing indoors or against a sunny wall outside. The bright yellow flowers show up well against its dark green, trifoliate leaves, and supported on a framework, this plant makes a good room divider. Alternatively it can be pruned into a bushy shape.*

Below left : Maranta leuconeura *needs a warm, moist atmosphere to produce a succession of new leaves. Spray clean water on the foliage from time to time to help keep it happy.*

Right : Hoya carnosa *is a climbing plant which although slow in starting, grows quite quickly once it is established. There is also a charming varie-gated variety of this plant as well as the green-leaved* H. bella *which produces even more brilliant wax-like flowers.*

47

Left : Beloperone Guttata *is a very decorative house plant with its lovely long-lasting yellow, orange and red bracts which hang gracefully on the plant. The flowers themselves are quite inconspicuous.*

Right : Monstera Deliciosa *produces this curious fruit, the edible part of which is the pulp around the spalix which is seen developing in this example. This is an easy plant to grow which produces abundant aerial roots that can be tied together and inserted into the soil.*

Left : Palms such as this Howea belmoreana *are both decorative and very long-lived. They appear to grow best when their roots are restricted and so they should not be repotted frequently. Pot-bound plants will need more water than those which have plenty of soil between their roots.*

Right : Anthurium scherzerianum *is known as the Piggy-tail Plant because of its curly spadices. These are quite tough house plants which grow best in good light without which they will not flower. They dislike draughts and dry conditions.*

Below : *The indomitable* Aspidistra *which was once so common is now a rarity in some countries. It will struggle to live in adverse conditions but fed and well cared for it will make a handsome and decorative plant.*

Left : Geraniums have for generations been a favourite among house plants. This flowering variety is an example of P. domestium, the Royal Pelargonium, which is one of the most beautiful of the flowering indoor plants.

Above left : Cissus Antarctica, popularly called the Kangaroo Vine, can be grown climbing up a stake or as a trailing plant.

Above right : Hibiscus Rosa-sinensis or Chinese Rose is an attractive, small shrub, with exotic, trumpet-shaped flowers. This plant needs full sun in order to flower.

Right : The well-known Impatiens Petersiana is an easy-to-grow house plant which grows quickly and flowers profusely.

53

Left : Araucaria excelsa
or Norfolk Island Pine
is really a bonsai when
grown as a house plant.
Growing naturally, it
reaches a height of 100
to 150 feet. It is an easy
plant to grow if kept in
a cool room away from
draughts. In a warmer
atmosphere it becomes
quite sizeable and can be
used attractively in large
spaces.

Right : Citrus mitis
produces white fragrant
blooms which are
followed by a crop of
delightful small oranges
in the autumn. To ensure
fruit, pollinate by
transferring the pollen
with a fine brush. The
fruits are edible but
rather sour and they can
be used in mixing drinks
or if plentiful, in making
marmalade. Some people
prefer to leave the fruit
on the tree in the winter
months.

Caladiums The fragile-looking, delightfully shaped, variously coloured leaves of the caladiums make this one of the most beautiful of foliage plants. They are, however, among the most difficult to grow. So much so that they are worth treating as flowering pot plants, because they can usually only survive the winter in a heated greenhouse. *C. candidum*, which is the most popular, has almost transparent snowy-green leaves that are veined a delicate green. Attractive varieties are 'Mary Moir', with its pale-green leaves, heavily veined bottle green, with maroon flecks, 'Mrs F. M. Joyner' whose leaves are rose centred with edges of dark green, 'Frieda Hemple', brilliant carmine with an avocado pear margin and 'Pink Beauty'. Illustrated in colour on pages 41 and 56.

CALAMONDIN ORANGE see *Citrus mitis.*

Calathea insignis see *Calathea mackoyana.*

Calathea louisae see *Calathea mackoyana.*

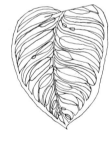

Calathea mackoyana

Calathea mackoyana PEACOCK PLANT This is the best known of the very decorative calatheas, which, having markings rather similar to the Marantas, are sometimes sold as such. It has very lovely silvery-green leaves with veins of dark green and edged with medium green. It is excellent for a bottle garden. All calatheas need to be kept very warm, in the shade and in a moist atmosphere. They should be well-watered during the summer, with considerably less in the winter. They do best in well drained, loose soil. Possibly easier to grow, but less colourful varieties are *C. insignis*, *C. ornata sanderiana* and *C. louisae.*

Calathea ornata sanderiana see *Calathea mackoyana.*

Calceolaria SLIPPER FLOWER or POCKETBOOK FLOWER Grown in pots, calceolaria usually flower in spring and summer and, after fading, are discarded. They are dwarf plants with large clusters of red, orange or yellow flowers, with distinctive markings and large, oval-shaped, pointed, rich green leaves. They need cool, airy, well-lit conditions, out of direct sunlight. A shady window-sill is ideal.

They should be watered freely and fed occasionally when in flower.

Callistemon citrinus BOTTLE BRUSH PLANT This plant from Australia, is a beautiful evergreen shrub. The variety 'Splendens' has brilliant scarlet flowers, with very colourful long stamens, over a long period. It grows in a cool room. It should be top-dressed, because it grows best when somewhat pot-bound.

Camellia japonica These evergreen, hardy shrubs with their handsome, glossy, dark-green leaves and delightful, wax-like flowers will grow for many years in quite small pots. They like much the same conditions as Indian azaleas, preferring a north facing window in a draught-free spot. Dryness, cold and draughts can cause the buds to drop off before blooming. They benefit quite considerably from being stood out of doors in a shady spot from early summer onwards. It is an excellent plan to buy a well-budded plant just after Christmas and have the pleasure of it in the house for about two months. If you want large flowers, pinch off all but one bud in each cluster. After flowering it is kept in a cool place and ultimately planted out, after it has been hardened off, when there is no more fear of frost.

Camellia

Campanula isophylla STAR OF BETHLEHEM This is a charming plant, which produces a cascade of either white or lilac-blue flowers. There is another beautiful form, *C. isophylla* 'Mayi', which has variegated foliage and delightful China-blue flowers. *C. isophylla* is really lovely when planted in a hanging pot. Unlike the majority of the members of its large family, it is not hardy and better grown indoors, where it should be given a cool, airy, draught-free, well-lit place. It needs good watering and feeding in summer, reducing it in the winter, when it should be kept at a temperature of 45-50°F (7-10°C). Illustrated in colour on page 24.

CANARY ISLAND IVY see *Hedera canariensis*, 'Variegata' and 'Golden Leaf'.

CAPE HEATH see *Erica*.

Capsicum annuum BIRD PEPPER This shrubby little plant with light green leaves bears small white flowers in summer followed by decorative cone-shaped berries which change from cream to red.

Calceolaria Darwinii. *The flowers of this type are elongated and less profuse than other varieties. Although these plants are usually discarded after flowering they can be grown from seeds sown in the summer.*

It does best in bright sunshine at normal room temperature. Water it freely in summer, spraying the leaves with clear water from time to time. Feed fortnightly throughout the spring and up until flowers form.

CAST IRON PLANT see *Aspidistra lurida.*

CASTOR OIL PLANT see *Fatsia japonica.*

CERIMAN see *Monstera deliciosa.*

Chamaedorea erumpens THE BAMBOO PALM This is a slender, but tall-growing palm which is suitable for a narrow alcove. It tolerates dry air, provided its roots are kept moist.

Chamaerops humilis FAN PALM This palm is almost hardy and easy to grow. It does best, therefore, in cool or only moderately warm rooms. It is an evergreen shrub, growing up to eight feet tall and producing a clump of stiff, fan-shaped leaves on long stems.

CHAMELEON see *Cryptanthus.*

CHESTNUT VINE see *Tetrastigma voinierianum.*

CHINESE EVERGREEN see *Aglaonema commutatum.*

CHINESE ROSE see *Hibiscus rosa-sinensis.*

Chlorophytum capense 'Variegatum' SPIDER PLANT This is among the easiest to grow and most tolerant of house plants. It grows as a dense tuft of arching leaves, rather like grass, that are edged bright green with a stripe of cream through the centre. Its insignificant white flowers are produced on long, corn-coloured stalks which stand above the plant. After flowering, small plantlets which look very much like spiders develop on them and these weigh them down, giving a pendulous or trailing effect and making the plant very effective for hanging baskets. The plant can be easily propagated by layering, i.e. by pinning these tiny tufts down in compost

Chamaedorea erumpens

Chamaerops humilis

with a hairpin and cutting them off when they have rooted.

This plant prefers a bright position, but not direct sunlight. It grows best in a medium humid place at a temperature of 65-75°F (18-24°C), with a drop of about 10°F at night. *C. capense* 'Variegatum' should be kept reasonably moist and never allowed to dry out. Re-potting into a slightly larger container annually is advantageous.

CHRISTMAS BEGONIA see *Begonias.*

CHRISTMAS CHERRY see *Solanum capsicastrum.*

Chrysanthemums Because of modern lighting techniques, potted chrysanthemums are now available in bloom throughout the year. Many of them are usually garden varieties that have been treated with dwarfing compounds to make them short-growing, bushy and compact. They all need to be stood in cool, well-lit, but sunless places, where there is a good air circulation. They should be watered regularly so that the soil does not dry out. It should be remembered that if any chrysanthemums that have been artificially dwarfed are subsequently planted out in the garden, they grow to a normal height.

Cineraria The large bouquet of daisy-like flowers surrounded by dark-green leaves makes this a very handsome but popular plant. It is difficult to surpass it for decorative beauty with its flowers of white, pink, blue or mauve. It is not a difficult plant if it is put in a cool, draught-free room with a good light away from direct sun. It should be well-watered and given an occasional feeding when it is flowering. It is usually thrown out after flowering.

Cissus antarctica KANGAROO VINE This is a very easy-to-grow, tough, fast-growing, self-clinging climber, reaching, if permitted, a height of eight feet. It is excellent, grown as a room divider. It has lovely, fresh-green, oval leaves, which are well-veined. It is easily propagated by layering.

Although it does best in good light, out of strong sun, it may also do fairly well in sunless and more shady rooms. It is quite tolerant of lower temperatures and will thrive at a temperature level of 50°F (10°C). It enjoys a medium humid atmosphere. It should be well watered at intervals during the summer and between waterings be allowed to dry out almost completely. It needs very little water during the winter. The variety 'Russikivin' is recommended. Illustrated in colour on page 53. *C. discolor* from Java which is

Below left : Chrysanthemums are always popular as flowering plants as the colours are particularly lovely against the medium-green leaves. When the plant has finished flowering, transfer it to the garden where it should bloom in the next season.

Below right : Cineraria is a very popular house plant because of the lovely colours of its bouquet-like cluster of flowers. It can be grown from seed, but is most often bought when it is a mature flowering plant. It is best to discard the plant after it has finished flowering. Greenfly can be a nuisance on Cinereria so be sure to examine the plant regularly for these pests.

aptly called the Rex Begonia Vine, has beautiful green, reddish-purple, mottled-white leaves. It is much less easy to grow than *C. antarctica,* and requires a much higher temperature and moist atmosphere to thrive. It has the disadvantage of tending to lose its leaves in winter, but this can be avoided if given the right conditions. *C. striata* from South America is very much more delicate than *C. antarctica* and needs more moisture, but it is useful because it is a smaller variety with neat, five-fingered leaves which takes up less room.

Cissus rhombifolia see *Rhoicissus rhomboidea.*

Citrus mitis CALAMONDIN ORANGE This unusual house plant often bears flowers and fruit simultaneously. It has white, sweet-scented blooms, and produces small bitter oranges. It, together with other orange species, is not difficult to grow. Most of all it needs plenty of sunshine. It benefits from ample water and regular feeding during the summer, with drier winter conditions. The temperature in winter should not be less than 50°F (10°C), but it can stand in the open from June until it becomes cold. Illustrated in colour on page 55.

Clivia miniata KAFFIR LILY A member of the Amaryllis family this is a spectacular, easy-to-grow house plant, with its strap-shaped, dark-green leaves and its dominating heads of orange flowers that are produced in the spring. It is claimed to be as tough and as long-lasting as the aspidistra. It should be kept dry and at a temperature above 45-50°F (7-10°C) in the winter, but it likes good watering, being sprayed, and occasional feeding during the summer months. It should be kept in a well-lit room, but away from direct sunlight. As it blooms best when pot-bound and dislikes root disturbance, it should only be re-potted when dire necessity arises.

Cocos weddelliana COCONUT PALM This palm grows slowly. It has very stiff, narrow leaves. It needs a minimum winter temperature of 70°F (21°C). As it likes shade, high humidity and moist soil, it thrives in a bottle garden.

Cocus weddelliana

Codiaeum variegatum CROTON or SOUTH SEA LAUREL This plant is distinguished by its brilliant foliage, and is vertical-growing and single-stemmed. The leaves are deeply veined, varying in shape, sometimes straight, other times twisted and variously patterned with orange, yellow, red, green and black. Crotons are difficult to acclimatize and need to be in a continuously centrally-heated, humid room, free from draughts with plenty of light.

C. variegatum pictum is an excellent plant for a bottle garden. Its very colourful cultivars are red and crimson *chelsoni*; the 'Blood Red Croton'; Pennick, orange-pink *reidii*; *thompsonii*, which is gold, chocolate and crimson and green; crimson and magenta *williamsii*. *C. van ostenzee* is a slow grower with dainty narrow variegated yellow and green leaves. Other attractive crotons are 'Emperor Alexander II' and 'Madame Mayne'.

As crotons become older, they often lose their leaves. This can be remedied by air-layering.

Coleus FLAME NETTLE This is a plant that is usually expendable. It has the most beautiful multi-coloured leaves. It is difficult to grow because it needs to be kept in well-lit draught-free rooms, at a temperature never below 55°F (13°C) in a continuously humid atmosphere. The leaves of the very beautiful 'Rainbow Strain' rival many flowers in colour.

Columnea banksii This climber needs a warm room in which the winter temperature does not fall below 55°F (13°C). It requires plenty of water during the growing period, but the soil should not be kept continuously saturated. The atmosphere should be kept humid by surrounding its pot with damp peat. It likes a well-lit place out of direct sunlight. Its massed, reddish-orange flowers are three inches long and an inch and a half wide, and tubular in shape. It is a difficult plant to grow, but perseverance aimed at getting the right conditions is richly rewarded.

Another glorious columnea is *C. gloriosa* 'Purpurea', which has the very exotic-looking, orange flowers and small, dark-purple, hairy leaves.

Cordyline terminalis FLAMING DRAGON TREE or TI PLANT There is some confusion about the botanical classification of this plant. It is additionally known as *Dracaena baptistii*, *D. terminalis*, *D. indivisa* and is often sold by florists as a 'Dracaena'. Whatever it is called,

Above left : The variegated foliage of Ctenanthe Oppenheimiana Tricolor makes it an attractive house plant which prefers a shady, warm and moist position and grows well in a bottle garden.

Above right : Cordyline Terminalis has bright pink or cerise foliage which is a lovely contrast to the green leaves of most house plants. It is quite easy to grow.

however, it has pink, cerise, or cream, oval young leaves, that eventually become mainly green and red with splashings and margins of these brighter colours. Its palm-like leaves are much sought after by flower arrangers. It is relatively easy to grow in an average light room. If the lower leaves fall as it grows older, this can be remedied by air-layering. They are tough plants and withstand all manner of abuse.

CREEPING MOSS see *Selaginella*.

CRESTED LADDER FERN see *Nephrolepsis exaltata*.

CROTON see *Codiaeum variegatum*.

Cryptanthus STARFISH PLANT, STAR PLANT and, because its leaves change colour on moving in and out of the sun, CHAMELEON. These are all low bromeliads that are easy to grow, provided they are given good light and not too much water. The two most common species are *C. bivittatus* with nine-inch long, evergreen leaves, with sharply toothed edges and two yellow bands running along their length and *C. zonatus*, that has alternative green and silvery-grey

Croton

This group of Cryptanthus planted as a dish garden shows the wide variety of foliage available in this plant. C. Zonatus with its stripy leaves contrasts with the solid-colour convoluted leaves of C. Aucalis and the striations of C. Bivittatus.

bands across its leaves of similar length, which are whitish underneath. Also there are *C. tricolor*, with cream stripes diffused with pink, and mottle-leaved *C. fosteriana*.

One of the most attractive ways of displaying *Cryptanthus* is to allow them to grow on an old log or piece of bark, as they do in nature, rather than in a pot. To do this, the plant should be removed from its container and its roots wrapped in a ball of fresh sphagnum moss. This should then be tied to the wood. The plant is watered either by spraying the moss covering or by plunging the plant plus its anchorage into a bucket of lukewarm water. *C. zonatus* needs fair moisture during the summer season, without over-watering. Cool winter temperatures do no harm, but little watering is necessary.

Cryptanthus bivittatus see *Cryptanthus*.
Cryptanthus fosteriana see *Cryptanthus*.
Cryptanthus zonatus see *Cryptanthus*.

Ctenanthe lubbersiana This plant from South America has very attractive, narrow leaves about eight inches long, which have their undersides pale green with their upper surface a deep green, variegated with yellow. In bright sunshine, which it dislikes, the edges of its leaves roll up. It needs a shady, warm and moist position for success, and is good in a bottle garden.

Cuphea hyssopifolia BARBADOS HEATHER This is one of the best house plants for continuous flowering. It makes a small, twiggy shrub with every twig covered with leaves, about one inch long and a quarter inch across. From the axils of these leaves emerge innumerable small purple trumpet-shaped flowers. Flowering starts in April or early May and will go on non-stop until Novem-

Another variety of Ctenanthe, C. Lubbersiana has good-looking variegated foliage which curls up at the edges if the plant is put in bright sunshine. It is another good plant for use in a bottle garden.

ber. During the winter a temperature of 55°F (13°C) is advisable. It likes a well-lit situation and does not mind some direct sunlight, so long as it is not excessively burning. During the winter it likes a well-lit situation.

CUPID'S BOWER see *Achimenes*.

CURLY FERN see *Nephrolepsis exaltata*.

Cyclamen persicum PERSIAN VIOLET This winter-flowering plant, with its heart-shaped, grey, green, silver or mottled leaves and profusion of white, pink, salmon-pink, crimson or cerise flowers, ranks with azaleas for beauty among flowering pot plants. It prolongs the display of winter colour for some weeks after the latter have faded.

Unfortunately, not everybody finds it easy to grow, because it dislikes a dry atmosphere and requires an atmosphere which does not rise above 50°F (10°C) in temperature. It should be regularly watered but always by standing the pot in water so that the crown is not wetted, otherwise it will rot. It likes to be fed regularly during flowering; and to be dead-headed continuously while in flower.

It is possible to make *C. persicum* available the following winter. After flowering, the watering should be lessened and feeding stopped. In the spring the pot should be put out into the garden in a shady position and brought into the house in late summer. If it has to be re-potted, the corm should stand out slightly above the surface. The soil used should be lime-free compost. A very attractive variety is *C. persicum* 'Rose Van Aalsmeer'.

Cyperus alternifolius SEDGE or UMBRELLA PLANT Being a swamp lover, it cannot be over-watered. It is easy to grow and will thrive in an unheated area. It has grass-like leaves emanating from its base, from which it also produces tall flowering stems which are dominated by crowns of shorter leaves, giving the appearance of an umbrella.

Cyrtomium falcatum HOUSE HOLLY FERN or SHIELD FERN This almost hardy fern is most valuable because it grows well in an ordinary living-room, providing it does not cool to too great an extent at night. It has shining, dark-green, toothed leaves that make it a fine, decorative plant that contrasts well with the more delicate-looking ferns that are grown indoors.

Below left : Cyclamen Persicum *available in an array of bright colours, is one of the loveliest of the flowering pot plants. Many people discard this plant once it has finished flowering, but it is possible to keep it through the summer with care and experience.*

Below right : Cyperus Alternifolius Variegata *is a graceful foliage plant which provides a contrast in leaf shape to more ordinary house plants. It is one of those fortunate plants which cannot be overwatered as it is a swamp grower naturally.*

Cyrtomium falcatum

DATE PALM see *Phoenix dactylifera.*
DEVIL'S IVY see *Scindapsus aureus.*
Dieffenbachia amoena see *Dieffenbachia picta.*
Dieffenbachia arvida see *Dieffenbachia picta.*
Dieffenbachia exotica see *Dieffenbachia picta.*
Dieffenbachia picta DUMB CANE, MOTHER-IN-LAW PLANT Most dieffenbachias are tall, handsome plants with prominently marked leaves. They all need a fairly high and constant temperature and, provided good humidity is present, they do well in a centrally-heated room. Although deep shade might reduce their variegation, they do better in a shady position. They need good watering in the summer, with considerable reduction in winter. Their large leaves should be sprayed with water every ten days. Their sap is poisonous and will cause great pain and swelling if it gets into one's mouth. Children and pets should not have access to them. *D. picta* has dark-green, pointed oblong leaves, covered with white and pale-green spots. Its cultivar 'Rudolph Roehrs' is mottled pale and dark green. *D. exotica (arvida)* has large, irregular markings of creamy white and *D. amoena* with its white feathering on immense, glossy, green leaves can be a valuable asset in any decor. If they lose their lower leaves, air-layering can correct this.
Dizygotheca elegantissima see *Aralia elegantissima.*
Dracaena DRAGON PLANT All dracaenas are very lovely, comparatively tall, slow-growing, foliage plants. Most species have long, firm, silky, long-lasting, pointed leaves, that are variously striped. Most of them shed their lower leaves as they grow taller, but this is not to their disadvantage. While they grow under average conditions, they are at their best in centrally heated rooms in which the temperature is never lower than 55°F (13°C) and the humidity is reasonably low. They need to be well watered in the summer, but this must be reduced during winter. Generally dracaenas do well in both bright and medium light, but direct sunlight is beneficial to the variegated types. There are two more dwarf dracaenas, which are very attractive in the house. *D. godseffiana*, which is one of the shorter growing types, has dark-green leaves with pale-yellow spots. *D. sanderi (D. sanderiana)*, which is smaller than most, is very attractive with its grey-green leaves, bordered with a white band. It thrives in semi-shade. Its colouring makes it a particularly

Below left : Dieffen-bachia Picta *is a common house plant which adds height and variety to a grouping of foliage plants. If the plant tends to lose its lower leaves as is sometimes the case, correct by a method called air-layering.*

Below right : Dracaena Deremensis Warnecki *is another attractive foliage pot plant which is a member of the bromeliad family. The central vase should be kept filled with water.*

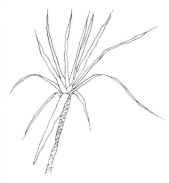

Dracaena marginata

good plant for dish and bottle gardens.

Among the larger types are *D. deremensis* 'Warnecki', which has grey-green leaves with two silver stripes and *D. deremensis* 'Bausei', with its dark-green leaves with a broad central stripe of white, growing from silvery coloured stems. Others are *D. fragrans*, which has broad, strap-shaped leaves with a gold band down their centres, *D. marginata*, which is perhaps a little easier to grow than the rest and has dull red-margined leaves, 'Firebrand' which is unusual but very lovely, with its narrow pink and red leaves, and lastly 'Red Edge' with its green leaves edged with pinkish-red.

Dracaena baptistii see *Cordyline terminalis.*
Dracaena deremensis 'Bausei' see *Dracaena.*
Dracaena deremensis 'Warnecki' see *Dracaena.*
Dracaena 'Firebrand' see *Dracaena.*
Dracaena fragrans see *Dracaena.*
Dracaena godseffiana see *Dracaena.*
Dracaena indivisa see *Cordyline terminalis.*
Dracaena marginata see *Dracaena.*
Dracaena sanderi see *Dracaena.*
Dracaena sanderiana see *Dracaena.*
Dracaena terminalis see *Cordyline terminalis.*
DRAGON PLANT see *Dracaena.*
DUMB CANE see *Dieffenbachia picta.*

Erica CAPE HEATH There are several very colourful cape heaths that appear as pot plants in the winter, representative of several hundred that flourish in South Africa. Unfortunately they are not hardy enough to withstand the winter out of doors and are difficult to grow indoors because they drop their leaves when the conditions do not suit them. They must have good light, a cool situation away from draughts, and plenty of water, preferably rain or soft water, so that the soil never dries out. The atmosphere surrounding the plant must be kept moist.

Erica

Exacum affine GERMAN VIOLET Small, fragrant yellow-centred, blue flowers cover this plant which has bright green leaves. It thrives at normal room temperature and likes all the sun it can get. Give it plenty of water in summer and feed fortnightly throughout the growing season. This plant is grown as an annual and plants are raised from seed or cuttings.

FAN PALM see *Chamaerops humilis*.

FAT-HEADED LIZZIE see *Fatshedera lizei*.

Fatshedera lizei FAT-HEADED LIZZIE, IVY TREE This plant, which is a cross between an English ivy and an aralia, has the characteristics of both its parents. It will grow eight feet tall or more, but it can be kept bushy by pinching out the leader. Its leaves, which have the texture and colour of the fatsia, have the shape of the ivy. It is easy to grow in cold and average rooms, particularly as it needs no winter heat. It should be well watered in the summer, but not excessively so, because this tends to brown the leaf edges. Direct sunlight tends to make its leaves wilt. *F. lizei* 'Variegata' is an attractive plant that is a great favourite of flower arrangers.

Fatshedera lizei 'Variegata' see *Fatshedera lizei*.

Fatsia japonica ARALIA, CASTOR OIL PLANT This large-growing plant is happy in cold and average rooms, is excellent for an entrance hall. In average sized rooms, it can be kept bushy by topping it in the spring. It is a very valuable accent plant, with its large, glossy green, round leaves, which have up to seven or nine blunt points.

Ficus ORNAMENTAL FIG There is little doubt that ficus are the most popular among the house plants. This is because of the dramatic effect that they can impart to the decor of modern rooms.

Ficus benjamina WEEPING FIG, WILLOW FIG This plant has the most fascinating ovate leaves, that quite abruptly terminate in a sharp point, closely clothing its graceful, drooping branches. It is not easy to grow, needing a well-lit, warm room, in which the temperature never falls below 50°F (10°C). It must not be over-watered,

Above left : Fatsia Japonica *is the familiar Castor Oil Plant. It grows best in cold rooms and does well on a patio or balcony as long as there is no deep frost. Keep it bushy by topping it in the spring to encourage new growth from below.*

Above right : Erica Snowfall *is a lovely variety of cape heath that is suitable for use as a pot plant. These plants are fairly fussy about the growing conditions so keep them in a room that is cool and well lit.*

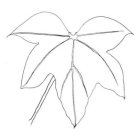

Fatshedera

particularly in the winter when it partially rests and may lose some leaves. If it becomes too dry, however, it wilts.

Ficus elastica 'Decora' INDIA RUBBER PLANT This is probably the best known and easiest to grow ficus and has taken the place of the Victorian aspidistra in modern living. Being hardy, it adapts itself to both warm and cold conditions, but it prefers to be in a room in which the temperature never fluctuates or falls below 50°F (10°C) in the winter, and there is not too much sunshine. It appreciates generous summer watering and liquid feeding, with less watering in the winter. It enjoys having its leaves washed frequently in luke-warm water. It is happier when planted in a small pot.

Fatsia japonica

It grows dignified, large, shiny, leathery, dark-green leaves, that first appear clothed in a red sheath, almost like a flower. Although it grows six to eight feet tall, it can be kept smaller by being cut back in the spring. Its tall growth and tolerance to cooler conditions make it an excellent specimen for shops, hotels and offices. Although rather more difficult to grow, its variegated counterpart, *F. elastica* 'Tricolor' with its leaves of pink, silvery-grey, cream and green is a very beautiful house plant. *F. elastica* 'Robusta' is regarded by some as better and more robust than 'Decora'.

Ficus elastica 'Robusta' see *Ficus elastica* 'Decora'.

Ficus lyrata, F. pandurata FIDDLE LEAF FIG, FIDDLE LEAF The leathery leaves of this large handsome house plant, which eventually grow eighteen inches long, are in the shape of a violin. They are strikingly marked with cream-coloured veins. Although a little more difficult to grow, it reacts to much the same handling as *F. elastica* 'Decora'. It is superb in a spacious hall.

Ficus pandurata see *Ficus lyrata.*

Ficus pumila CREEPING FIG This is a very attractive, small, hardy

Below left : Ficus Benjamina *is another variety of fig with smaller leaves and a tree-like shape. This variety is quite temperamental and needs a warm, well-lit room. It is essential not to over-water or it will lose its leaves.*

Below right : Ficus Elastica Decora, *the popular India Rubber Plant, is a familiar sight in homes and offices.*

climbing or trailing plant, which has small, bright-green leaves with their veins of a much darker hue. It is easy to grow. It produces aerial roots, which cling to a moss stick or, in fact, a rough surface such as a piece of bark, or the outside walls of a container. It is excellent for hanging baskets or for trailing over the edge of dishes. It is easily propagated by layering.

It is a particularly unusual plant because it prefers cool or average rooms. It dislikes direct sun, revels in moist air and must be well watered and never allowed to dry out even in the winter.

Ficus radicans 'Variegata' is very attractive for a hanging basket, but it is a difficult plant and must be kept in a very moist atmosphere. The temperature of its environment should never be lower than 50°F (10°C). Its rather beautiful, small, green and white leaves make it worth growing.

Ficus schryveriana. The leaves of this hardy, bushy ficus which are green and yellow, are smaller than those of *F. elastica* 'Decora'.

FIDDLE LEAF FIG see *Ficus lyrata*.

FIG LEAF PALM see *Fatsia japonica*.

FIG (ORNAMENTAL) see *Ficus*.

FINGER ARALIA see *Aralia elegantissima*.

FISHBONE PLANT see *Maranta leuconeura* 'Erythrophylla'.

Fittonia Argyroneura *has interestingly marked leaves, the white veins of which stand out in contrast to the rest. Reproduce it from cuttings taken in the spring, and plant in smallish pots.*

Fuchsia *Evensong*. *These delicate flowers need a good background to show them off; a large and dark leafed plant or plants is often the most effective, and will also absorb the rather woody stems and paler leaves of the Fuchsia.*

Fittonia argyroneura SNAKE SKIN PLANT This attractive, low-growing plant has oval leaves, coloured medium green with white veins, which combine together to give the plant an attractive bluish-green appearance. It is a difficult house plant to grow outside a bottle garden, because it has a constant need of humidity and warmth, but it cannot stand great heat or direct sunlight. It requires a minimum temperature of 55°F (13°C). While it should not be allowed to get too dry, overwatering is also detrimental and a careful balance must be maintained. When outside a bottle keep the plant away from draughts and plunge its pot into damp peat.

Fittonia verschaffeltii is a very beautiful trailer with smallish, heart-shaped, dark-green leaves, criss-crossed with a network of crimson veins. It is best suited to a bottle garden or terranium but can be used in a hanging basket.

FLAME NETTLE see *Coleus*.

FLAMING DRAGON TREE see *Cordyline terminalis*.

FLAMINGO PLANT see *Anthurium scherzerianum*.

FRIENDSHIP PLANT see *Pilea cadierei*.

FRUIT SALAD PLANT see *Monstera deliciosa*.

Fuchsia LADY'S EARDROPS The fuchsia produces fat or slender bell-shaped flowers like ballet skirts. The colours range from deep purple through scarlet, rosy red, pink, orange and white and there are even some with bluish tints. The plant grows best in good light in airy conditions but will tolerate semi-shade. Water it freely throughout the summer but keep soil dryish in winter when plants resting. Feed plants fortnightly during the spring and summer. To encourage new growth prune back shoots in late winter, early spring and re-pot in fresh soil, watering well. Raise new plants from stem cuttings or from seeds.

GERANIUMS see *Pelargoniums*.
GERMAN VIOLET see *Exacum affine*.
GLOIRE DE LORRAINE see *Begonias*.
Gloxinia Being essentially a greenhouse plant, gloxinia growing in a house need to be put in a warm spot, out of the full sun, with a moist atmosphere and soil that is always kept moist. Watering should always be done from the bottom so that the flowers and foliage are not damaged. It likes regular feeding during flowering. It has large, velvety, trumpet-shaped flowers, which, according to the variety, are rich crimson, deep red, white, violet and various combinations of such colours, and very beautiful, long, broad, pointed, downy, mid-green leaves. A very beautiful plant, which is representative of this large range is 'Emperor Frederick'.
GOOSE FOOT see *Syngonium podophyllum*.

Gloxinia

Grevillea robusta SILK OAK or AUSTRALIAN WATTLE This plant is wrongfully regarded by some people as a fern, because of its very pleasing, silvery-green, finely divided foliage. It is, however, less trouble to grow in an ordinary living room than most ferns so it has become a much appreciated substitute. It is most adaptable, requiring neither warmth in the winter nor a humid atmosphere, it does not, however, like cold draughts. It must not be allowed to dry out otherwise its leaves fall. Eventually outstripping any house room for size, it is marvellous decoration for an office, showroom or hotel foyer. It grows easily from seeds.
Gynura VELVET PURPLE PLANT The velvety leaves of this attractive plant are a regal purple. It is a multi-purpose plant, making both an excellent trailer or a bushy house plant. It is converted into the latter by pinching out the points of the shoots. It can also be trained up small canes and then becomes an attractive climber, reaching a height of eighteen inches. It is also beautiful in a hanging basket, if it is allowed to grow loosely over the edge. It appreciates central heating, good lighting and plenty of water in the summer.
Gynura sarmentosa produces unpleasant-smelling, orange flowers that must be picked off.

Gynura

HART'S TONGUE FERN see *Phyllitis scolopendrium*.
Hedera IVY These are the most valuable of all climbing and trailing house plants and can be most effectively employed for all the functions of this type of plant. They can be planted in baskets, to grow over the edge of bowls, to climb supports of bamboo canes, and as room dividers. It is also becoming the vogue to grow indoors ivy standard plants, using fatshedera as root stock. Although it takes some time to achieve because, to be really attractive, the stem should be three to four feet tall, it is not difficult for a 'do-it-yourself' gardener to create his own ivy standard. This is done by first cutting back all the shoots from a fatshedera, except one which is growing more or less vertically, staking it and removing all but the top growth until it has reached the required height. The top of the plant is then cut off and a horizontal cut, half an inch deep,

is made across the cross-section of the stem. Four cuttings of ivy, each about four inches long, are inserted into this and they are bound in with raffia or plastic tape.

There is little difficulty in the cultivation of ivies. The first essential is that they are grown in a good, moisture-retaining soil, which contains some rotted compost or peat. They do like, however, to have it a little on the acid side. They should never be allowed to dry out, although the water supply should be reduced in the winter. They do not like bright light, warm conditions or constantly dry air. Spraying their leaves is very beneficial. Hederas prefer to be grown in small pots.

Hedera canariensis 'Golden Leaf' This variety of ivy has a lightish green centre to its bright green leaves with red stems and stalks.

Hedera canariensis 'Variegata' CANARY ISLAND IVY This is another species which is most popular as a house plant. During the winter the interesting colour of *H. canariensis* 'Variegata' can be preserved by putting it into a well-lit position.

Hedera helix COMMON IVY This common ivy species, with its deep-green, shiny leaves, makes an excellent house plant. Some of its varieties and those of other species, with their bright colours, and differently shaped, smaller leaves, are even better.

Hedera helix 'Adam' This plant has grey-green, variegated, perfectly shaped, tiny leaves, closely packed to the extent of overlapping on the stems. Care should be taken not to wet the centre of the plant, otherwise rotting is likely to occur.

Hedera helix 'Chicago' This ivy has small, dark-green leaves, often stained bronze-purple.

Hedera helix 'Cristata' HOLLY IVY This is a distinctive form of ivy. It has pale-green leaves that are rather charmingly twisted and crinkled at the edges. It has been likened to parsley and likes to be kept drier than other varieties.

Hedera helix 'Glacier' This is one of the most effective of the 'silver' ivies with its small, silvery-grey leaves with thin, white margins.

Hedera helix 'Golden Jubilee'. The leaves of this ivy are small and

Below left : Hedera Helix *Glacier is a lovely variety of ivy with delicately shaped silvery grey-green foliage. You can train it to grow on a trellis to make a striking room divider, or use it as a trailing plant in a hanging basket or window box.*

Below right : Grevillea Robusta *is a lovely evergreen shrub which makes an attractive house plant. It has finely divided and delicate foliage which resembles some types of fern, and can grow very tall in the right growing conditions.*

golden, with a broad, dark-green margin, which makes it unusual.
Hedera helix 'Sagittifolia' This variety has leaves that are five-lobed, the central one of which is large and triangular. They are small and dark green, and have slightly white veins.
Hedera helix 'Shamrock' This variety has small, very dark-green leaves.
Helxine soleirolii MIND YOUR OWN BUSINESS, BABY'S TEARS and IRISH or JAPANESE MOSS This is a charming dwarf plant that creeps over the ground in Corsica. Fantastically easy to grow, it is a water-lover and one of the few indoor plants that can flourish when its pot is kept standing in a saucer of water. It grows in deep shade. The foliage must not, however, be wetted in winter, because it is liable to rot. It is a most valuable house plant because it can carpet the soil beneath either a single plant or a group.
Hibiscus rosa-sinensis CHINESE ROSE This evergreen shrub is a bushy plant with dark-green, glossy leaves and colourful flowers, that measure up to five inches across. There are whites, pinks, reds, oranges and yellows with some blooms single and others double. There is also a very pretty cultivar, *H. rosa-sinensis* 'Cooperi', which has variegated leaves of deep green and light yellow, tinged reddish-pink. Hibiscus thrive in a well-lit room, with full sun when blooming. In the winter, they should be kept fairly dry in a place where the temperature does not fall below 50°F (10°C). During the growing season, they should be well watered and fed occasionally. The plant should be sprayed occasionally to keep the air moist. In early spring hibiscus are pruned to induce good bud formation. Illustrated in colour on page 53.
HOUSE HOLLY FERN see *Cyrtomium falcatum.*
Howea belmoreana, Kentia belmoreana CURLY PALM This species and *H. forsteriana* KENTIA PALM are generally considered the best palms for growing in pots and for use in living-rooms. The temperature during the winter should not fall below 45°F (7°C) for both of them. They eventually become large and tall and need a

Howea

Below left : Another charming variety of ivy is Hedera Helix *Chicago which is best suited as a trailing plant. It has small, nicely-shaped leaves outlined in cream which give the plant a light and delicate look.*

Below right : Hydrangea Hortensis *is an effective flowering plant indoors and out and is available in a variety of pastel colours from blues and lavenders to pinks and white.*

Above left : Hoya
Carnosa *produces
bunches of waxy,
fragrant white or pink
flowers. Prune the plant
lightly to keep it tidy.*

Above right : Hoya Bella
*is a dramatic plant when
in bloom. It grows best
when trained up a stake
or around a window
frame so that the clusters
of flowers hang decora-
tively around it.*

large pot. They both have graceful, feathery leaves. Illustrated in
colour on page 50.

Howea forsteriana see *Howea belmoreana.*

Hoya australis see *Hoya carnosa.*

Hoya carnosa WAX PLANT, PORCELAIN FLOWER This is an easy-to-
grow climbing plant with glossy, fleshy leaves and clusters of pale-
pink, sweetly scented flowers that appear in summer. To be successful, it must have warmth and plenty of water when in flower. When
the plant is growing it needs to be watered freely and given an
occasional feeding. When the plant is at the flower-bud stage, feeding should be stopped and watering reduced very considerably.
It can stand cold conditions in the winter, but it flowers best in
the shade where it is warm. There is a very beautiful variegated
variety, *H. carnosa* 'Variegata', which has cream and green leaves;
is another rather slower-growing variety. Another attractive species
is *H. australis*, which has pink, flushed, white, honeysuckle-
scented flowers. Illustrated in colour on page 47.

Hoya carnosa 'Variegata' see *Hoya carnosa.*

HUSBAND AND WIFE see *Maranta leuconeura* 'Kerchoreana'.

Hydrangea hortensis The florist's hydrangea has very large, usually
single or occasionally double ball-headed blooms on short stems
around nine inches high. The flowers are shades of blue, red, pink
and white. Give it a cool light airy position when in flower and feed
weekly with diluted liquid fertilizer to prolong the display. Blooms
appear over the winter period. You can change pink varieties to a
deep, ultramarine-blue by adding a teaspoonful of alum to the pot
soil and watering this in. After flowering, shorten the shoots to
leave one or two pairs of leaves above the older wood. Continue to
feed and water to sustain new growth. Set the plant outdoors in a
lightly shaded spot for the summer and bring indoors in September
for plant to flower again. Raise new plants from stem cuttings in
early summer. Illustrated in colour on page 43.

Hoya bella

Impatiens petersiana BUSY LIZZIE, PATIENCE PLANT, PATIENT LUCY
This plant produces flowers, which are more usually pink, nearly the whole year round. It grows quickly. It must have a sunny position when in flower, otherwise it needs a well-lit position out of the sun, and to be kept warm in the winter, when it should be maintained just moist enough to prevent the leaves from wilting. In summer, it should be given ample water and be fed regularly. It pays also to spray it overhead, but as the plant is subject to attacks of mildew, this practise should be discontinued in the winter. To keep it bushy, it can be periodically pinched back. In addition to several dwarf forms, which include 'Baby Grange' and 'Baby Scarlet', there are some very attractive taller varieties, including 'Red Herald', which has large scarlet flowers marked with white. It can be very easily propagated from cuttings. Illustrated in colour on page 53.

INDIA RUBBER PLANT see *Ficus elastica* 'Decora'.
INDOOR LIME TREE see *Sparmannia africana*.
IRISH MOSS see *Helxine soleirolii*.
IRON CROSS BEGONIA see *Begonias*.
IVY see *Hedera*.
IVY TREE see *Fatshedera lizei*.

JAPANESE MOSS see *Helxine soleirolii*.
JASMINE see *Jasminum mesnyi*.
Jasminum mesnyi JASMINE This is one of those very valuable dual-purpose plants. It is equally comfortable growing indoors or against a warm, sunny wall outdoors where it will reach a height of fifteen feet or more. Because of this quality, it can be stood outside during the summer or be safely transplanted into a warm position in the garden, if a change of decor makes it redundant. The very lovely, bright yellow flowers show up well against its dark-green, trifoliate leaves. Supported on a framework, it makes a good room divider, or pruning will keep it bushy. Illustrated in colour on page 46.
Jasminum polyanthum, which resembles the white garden jasmine, is a beautiful climber. It has white, highly perfumed flowers, pink on the outside, and dark green leaves like *J. mesnyi*. It should be kept in a fairly moist atmosphere, at not less than 45°F (7°C) in

Above left : This large Impatiens Petersiana *has been pruned into a graceful shape. These plants are easy to grow and can be expected to flower for much of the year. Cuttings root easily and quickly in water.*

Above right : Lauris Nobilis *or Bay Tree makes a useful and good-looking indoor shrub which can be pruned into a compact shape or allowed to grow at will. The leaves when dried are used in cookery as an addition to stews and patés.*

Jasmine is a popular house plant which produces lovely blooms in early spring and can be successfully grown as a hanging plant.

the winter and in a sunny place. Its size, like that of *J. mesnyi*, can be controlled by stopping its shoots during the growing season.
Jasminum primulinum see *Jasminum mesnyi*.
JOSEPH'S COAT see *Scindapsus aureus*.

KAFFIR LILY see *Clivia miniata*.
Kentia belmoreana see *Howea belmoreana*.
KENTIA PALM see *Howea belmoreana*.

LADY'S EARDROPS see *Fuchsia*.
LADY PALM see *Rhapis excelsa*.
Lauris nobilis BAY TREE This evergreen, the leaves of which are prized by cooks, makes an excellent and useful indoor shrub. It will succeed in any normal soil, but it is a lover of full sun. Its size can be kept under control by careful trimming or by picking the leaves for drying for storage.
LIPSTICK VINE see *Aeschyanthus speciosus*.
LIZARD PLANT see *Tetrastigma voinierianum*.

Jasminium officinale

PEACOCK PLANT see *Calathea makoyana*.

MAIDENHAIR FERN see *Adiantum cuneatum*.

Maranta The plants in this group are not easy to grow because they need warmth, shade, root moisture and humidity. They are excellent for bottle gardens and terrariums because of their very ornamental foliage. Similarly, they can give a dramatic effect to the simplest dish garden.

Maranta leuconeura

Maranta leuconeura 'Erythrophylla' Tricolor This attractive variety has bright-green leaves with red and brown markings. Illustrated in colour on page 46.

Maranta leuconeura 'Kerchoveana' PRAYER PLANT, HUSBAND AND WIFE The first common name of this plant comes from its habit of closing up its leaves at sundown. It is a delightful, bushy plant with prominent, reddish-brown blotches on either side of its centre veins.

Maranta leuconeura 'Massangeana' FISH BONE PLANT This maranta has leaves of soft green with the main veins picked out in white to give a herring-bone effect. The underside of the leaves is purple.

Maranta picturata has light-grey leaves with dark-green edges and maroon underneath. It is a difficult variety to grow.

Maranta Leuconeura Kerchoveana *has green leaves which are decoratively marked with red veins which stand in relief. In spring, propagate the plant by division and re-pot using well-drained, smallish pots.*

Maranta Tricolor see *Maranta leuconeura* 'Erythrophylla'.

MEXICAN BREADFRUIT see *Monstera deliciosa.*

MIND-YOUR-OWN-BUSINESS see *Helxine soleirolii.*

Monstera deliciosa SWISS CHEESE PLANT, MEXICAN BREADFRUIT, CERIMAN and FRUIT SALAD PLANT The popular names of this plant refer either to its curious leaf form or its fruit. It is a giant, handsome foliage plant that fortunately grows fairly slowly in a small pot; it can be kept down in height by cutting out its top periodically. Its enormous dark-green leaves are slashed and perforated in an almost startling fashion. Its new leaves, which are produced from a long cone-shaped bud attached to the stem of an old one, are very glossy and delicate green in colour. It produces abundant, long, aerial roots, which can beneficially be tied together and inserted in the soil in its pot. Another feature is that in time it produces a flower, followed by a delicious fruit with an elusive flavour between that of pineapple and banana.

Although it will adapt itself to cooler conditions, it likes warmth, good humidity, plenty of water and feeding during summer. The soil should be allowed to become fairly dry between waterings. Illustrated in colour on page 49.

Monstera pertusa. This giant foliage plant, when allowed to grow freely under favourable conditions, becomes one of the largest of the indoor plants. As a result, it is very popular for offices, shops, public buildings and other roomy places. Fortunately, it is most effective in a container, because due to the root restriction, it grows quite slowly. The height can be controlled by cutting out its top.

MOSES IN THE RUSHES see *Rhoeo discolor.*

MOTHER-IN-LAW PLANT see *Dieffenbachia picta.*

MOTHER-IN-LAW'S-TONGUE see *Sansevieria trifasciata* 'Laurentii'.

MOTHER OF THOUSANDS see *Saxifraga sarmentosa.*

Neanthe bella PARLOUR PALM or DWARF PALM This palm is regarded as the best and easiest for growing in the house. It is small, eventually reaching four feet high. The long pinnate and bright green leaves, hang gracefully making it attractive as a single specimen; it is excellent as the pinnacle in an arrangement and it adds charm to a bottle garden. It should be given a light position out of direct sunlight, watered freely in summer and sparingly in winter. It much appreciates having its leaves sponged or sprayed occasionally as it particularly dislikes a hot and dry atmosphere in which the leaves will turn brown. Another variety is *N. elegans*.

Neanthe elegans see *Neanthe bella*.

Neoregelias These bromeliads have striking, colourful foliage, particularly in their cup-like centres which, during the growing season, should be kept filled with tepid water, preferably rainwater. They have insignificant flowers that grow in these centres. When they fade they should be removed with tweezers and the cups washed out because otherwise they smell unpleasant. Neoregelias need well-lit quarters and a temperature that never falls below 50°F (10°C).

Neoregelia carolinae 'Tricolor' This is an easy bromeliad to grow. Its saw-toothed leaves, twelve to fifteen inches long and one to one and a half inches wide are green with an inner, lengthwise-running stripe of cream, becoming pink at their bases, where they form a cup-shaped depression, pink in colour. Just before the inconspicuous flowers appear, it becomes vivid scarlet. It prefers to be placed in the shade or semi-shade, but it does not mind a dry atmosphere. In summer, keep the cup full of tepid water.

Neoregelia marechali This plant is particularly attractive. It has broad, strap-like, bright-green leaves with spiny edges and a bright-red centre.

Nephrolepsis exaltata bostoniensis BOSTON FERN, CRESTED LADDER FERN, CURLY FERN, SWORD FERN, WHITMAN FERN The fronds of this beautiful fern are two feet long or even more, with leaflets (pinnae) up to three inches long and a half inch wide. It is stately and tall, which qualities are especially exemplified when grown on its own in a pot. Yet at the same time there is a smoothness about the manner in which its large fronds gracefully droop, that makes

Right : Nephrolepsis Exaltata *is one of the most commonly grown ferns which looks beautiful as a hanging plant with its fronds cascading down or standing in a pot. All ferns are difficult to grow indoors but it is well-worth trying as they are such lovely additions to any room.*

Below left : Neanthe Bella *is commonly known as the Parlour Palm and it is an elegant and easy-to-grow type of palm which stays fairly small and is an excellent subject for dish gardens when it is a young plant.*

Below right : Neoregelia Carolinae Tricolor *is a type of bromeliad and has dramatic pinky-cream striated foliage. Always keep the brilliant pink centre cup filled with water.*

it, either singly or with others, superb for growing in hanging baskets. It survives well in adverse conditions.

NEPHTHYTIS see *Syngonium podophyllum*.

Nerium oleander OLEANDER, ROSE BAY This shrub requires plenty of space. It is a very beautiful, willow-leaved plant, with clusters of fragrant, tubular flowers, measuring no less than three inches across, but every part of it is poisonous. It is deadly if eaten! The more usual colour is pink, but there are white, yellow and red varieties, and one with variegated leaves. Cuttings root very easily.

It needs a sunny position, with plenty of watering with tepid water, spraying and occasional feeding in the summer. Its wood can be ripened by standing outside as much as possible in the summer. Its winter temperature should not be allowed to fall below 50°F (10°C). Re-potting is done in February.

Nidularium fulgens BIRD'S NEST BROMELIAD This plant is an epiphytic bromeliad, which means that when it grows naturally it attaches itself to another plant. It is a native of Southern Brazil. The main, long, green leaves are about twelve inches long and two inches wide. In the centre there are six to ten short, scarlet leaves. After the rather insignificant flowers die, the centre of the rosette must be kept filled with water. An easy plant to grow in a pot, it does well without much light and should preferably be kept at a moderate, even temperature.

NORFOLK ISLAND PINE see *Araucaria excelsa*.

OLEANDER see *Nerium oleander*.

Oxalis WOOD SORREL This family of tuberous-rooted plants with clover-shaped leaves and various coloured flowers grow easily with minimum attention. They close up their leaves and flowers at night and on sunless days and tend to do the same if it is too hot or if they are allowed to become too dry. Some varieties are *O. orassipes* with small, purply-pink flowers, *O. henrei* which is evergreen and produces small yellow flowers and *O. melanostica* which is dormant in spring and summer producing yellow flowers and grey leaves in the autumn.

Below : Peperomias are members of the pepper family of which there are about 400 species, about a dozen being suited for indoor plants. Peperomia Caperata (right) has small, heart-shaped, corrugated leaves and produces white flower spikes. Peperomia Caperata Variegata is seen on the left.

PAINTED FEATHERS see *Vriesia splendens*.

PAINTER'S PALETTE see *Anthurium scherzerianum*.

Pandanus veitchii SCREW PINE This attractive foliage plant has palm-like leaves, that grow to two feet or even longer and are green in colour, bordered with white or silver-white, with vicious spines on the margins. The plant should be placed where it cannot be easily touched. The spines are spirally arranged on the stem which gives rise to the popular name. Because it demands constant warmth, not below 55°F (13°C) in the winter, a moist atmosphere and good light, out of direct sunshine, it is regarded as a difficult plant to grow. Spray the foliage frequently. It needs to be well watered during the summer, but it should be allowed to become fairly dry between waterings. It likes a small pot.

Above left : Pandanus Veitchii, *commonly known as the Screw Pine, is an ornamental plant with long, sword-shaped, spiny-edged leaves which are green with white stripes. Do not overwater this plant and propagate by means of offsets which can be removed in late spring.*

Above right : The ever-popular geranium is a versatile house plant which is an easy-to-grow evergreen and provides colourful and long-lasting displays of blooms in a wide variety of growing conditions.

PARLOUR PALM see *Neanthe bella*.

Passiflora caerulea PASSION FLOWER This plant is a quick-growing, hardy climber. Blue is the more common, but *P. caerulea* 'Constance Elliott' is a very delightful, white variety. A sunny position is needed. It should be given plenty of water during the summer and receive an occasional feed. The temperature should not fall below 50°F (10°C) in the winter. Keep under control by pruning hard in early spring. Illustrated in colour on page 42.

PASSION FLOWER see *Passiflora caerulea*.

PATIENCE PLANT see *Impatiens petersiana*.

PATIENT LUCY see *Impatiens petersiana*.

PEACE LILY see *Spathiphyllum wallisii*.

PEACOCK PLANT see *Calathea mackoyana*.

Pelargoniums GERANIUM There are many varieties of the different colours and leaf patterns of geranium with which most people are familiar. Their needs are pure air and a place in a warm, sunlit, dry, airy room. A window-sill facing south is ideal. Many types are attractive even when not flowering. Some varieties have scented leaves which give off a lovely fragrance. Ivy-leaved geraniums can be used as hanging plants with flowers that come in pink, white and shades of rose and purple. Illustrated in colour on page 52.

Pellaea rotundifola. This small fern is very effective in a bottle garden, hanging basket and pot. It forms rounded clumps and has eight to ten inch long fronds, that give off up to twenty stalks, each of which carry small, dark-green, round, secondary leaves.

Peperomias These are moderate or small plants with very lovely leaves and flowers, sometimes carried high on colourful stalks, which together make the plants extraordinarily decorative.

They all require warmth, humidity, some shade and, as they have small roots, to be grown in small, well-drained pots. At no time should they be excessively watered and should be kept rather drier in winter than is usual for plants kept under warm conditions. Feed fortnightly if the growth is poor. Spray the leaves to freshen them and keep them free from dust. They are very suitable for bottle gardens.

Peperomia argyreia see *Peperomia sandersii*.

Peperomia caperata is among the best known varieties. It has heart-shaped, dark-green, corrugated leaves on pink stems and curious, cream flowers, like shepherds' crooks, borne on light-brown stalks. It will grow in deep shade.

Peperomia hederifolia is similar to, but rather larger than, *P. caperata*. Its glossy leaves are less crinkled and metallic grey-green

Below left : Philoden-dron Bipennifolium *is a large-growing type of philodendron. The name 'philodendron' comes from the Greek and means 'tree lover' and many of these plants including* P. Bipenni-folium *are climbers which produce aerial roots.*

Below Right : Pepero-mia Magnoliaefolia *or Green Gold Peperomia has green oval leaves with cream markings and looks well as an addition to a dish garden of foliage plants.*

in colour. It is a little more delicate.

Peperomia magnoliaefolia GREEN GOLD This variety is a tough, but slower-growing, shrubby plant, which has brilliant cream and green leaves, borne on short, branching, reddish stems. It is similar to *P. obtusifolia*.

Peperomia obtusifolia see *Peperomia magnoliaefolia*.

Peperomia sandersii WATERMELON PEPEROMIA The shape of the leaves of this variety are dark-green crescents, patterned with silver. It forms a very lovely clump. It is the most beautiful of all the peperomias and is similar to *P. argyreia*.

PERSIAN VIOLET see *Cyclamen persicum*.

Philodendrons This group probably contains some of the best known foliage plants. It is difficult to find leaves of more beauty and with such variable and lovely shapes. These plants probably grow better in the conditions found in modern homes than any other house plants. Little harm comes to them if they are kept

Peperomia sandersii

warm, if possible in a temperature of not less than 65°F (18°C), moderately moist, are allowed to dry out between waterings, and out of direct sunlight. They are not difficult to grow, but their beauty is so rewarding that it is worth while giving them just that little extra care. While some are dwarf bush plants, many are climbers. The latter produce aerial roots.

Philodendron andreanum see *Philodendron melanochryson.*

Philodendron bipennifolium This variety has grey-green foliage and aerial roots. It is fairly easy to grow and is an attractive climber.

Philodendron bipinnatifidum. This bushy plant is not difficult to grow. The long, fleshy roots that emerge from its growing point should be trained back into the soil.

Philodendron 'Burgundy' This tolerant variety benefits very much from the support of a moist moss stick into which its aerial roots can penetrate. It assumes a rich hue from the reflection of the colour of its deep, wine-red stem in its superb two-foot long leaves. It grows fairly slowly.

Philodendron cordatum see *Philodendron scandens.*

Philodendron dubium This is a slow-growing bush that never gets out of hand.

Philodendron

Below left : Philodendron Melanochryson *is a small variety of this family. Train it to grow up a stake, or prune it into a pleasing compact shape as here. Its leaves are an interesting shade of dark-purple with a velvety surface.*

Below right : Philodendron Bipinnatifidum *is a compact non-climbing species. The leaves remain undivided for up to two years.*

Philodendron elegans This plant has charming divided foliage. It grows well in shade in an average room and does well as a climbing plant.

Philodendron erubescens The arrow-shaped leaves of this plant have a rosy tinge when young, becoming dark green and purplish. It makes aerial roots. It is fairly easy to grow in an average or warm room. It is a large plant and an attractive climber.

Philodendron laciniatum This variety is a climber with medium-sized, dark leaves.

Philodendron leichtinii An interesting, slender climber with fantastic, evenly slashed, oval leaves, this variety is difficult to grow, needing more heat and humidity than can be comfortably supplied in living-rooms.

Philodendron melanochryson This is a climber with small, dark-purple leaves and a velvet sheen. It grows aerial roots and needs a warm position continuously. The soil should be kept fairly dry in winter. It is similar to *P. andreanum*.

Philodendron oxycardium see *Philodendron scandens*.

Philodendron pertusum This bushy type of philodendron is like a smaller version of *Monstera deliciosa* and is often referred to as such.

Philodendron scandens SWEETHEART VINE or BATHROOM PLANT This variety is no doubt the most popular of the climbing philodendrons. It is certainly the easiest of all house plants for a beginner. It is an excellent plant for a dark room. Although it likes warm conditions, it will grow reasonably in a cool room. It is primarily a climbing plant and throws out many aerial roots, and is therefore ideal for climbing a moss stick. It can, nevertheless, be grown as a bushy plant if the leader is regularly pinched out. Because of its heart-shaped leaves, it is commonly called 'Sweetheart Vine'; it is also known as 'Bathroom Plant' which is a reflection of the living conditions it likes best. A very similar, but what appears to be a larger version of this plant, *P. cordatum* 'Totem Pole Philodendron', is also popular.

Philodendron selloum This very striking, sturdy, slow-growing, spreading philodendron has its very large leaves cut into strips half-way to the midrib. As they fall, they leave white scars on the stem, which add to its attractiveness. It is particularly resistant to cold and will stand freezing temperatures.

Philodendron wendlandi is tolerant of extremes of temperature and humidity. It is compact and has long, narrow leaves.

Above left : Pilea Microphylla *is a member of the nettle family and with its ornamental foliage it is an attractive plant to grow indoors. Propagation is easy from cuttings in the spring or early summer. Pinch out the growing tips of the plant to ensure busy growth and prevent the plant from becoming scraggly.*

Above right : This type of Philodendron, P. Leichtinii *is characterized by its dramatically cut-out leaves. Like other members of this family, it grows quite large and has to be supported.*

Right : Another popular fern to grow indoors is Phyllitis Scolopendrium *which is a hardy fern that grows wild. Its broad leaves with wavy edges are a medium green and look lovely with light shining through them. This fern is able to withstand quite cold rooms and so is easier to grow than other more delicate varieties.*

Phoenix dactylifera DATE PALM This palm grows up to sixty feet high in its natural surroundings, but makes a very lovely house plant when planted in a pot. Its leaves are a bright green. It can be raised from date stones.

Phoenix roebelenii is the species that is more often seen in florists. It is a very elegant and striking house plant. The leaves, which are feathery and shiny and dark green in colour, have leaflets that are sometimes sickle-shaped. The richness of its green can be retained by placing a lump of sulphate of iron on the surface of the soil and allowing it to dissolve during the course of watering. It needs to be kept warmer than *P. dactylifera*. Its winter temperature should not fall below 60°F (15°C).

Phyllitis scolopendrium, Scolopendrium vulgare HART'S TONGUE FERN This is a hardy fern that grows wild. There are quite a few varieties grown as house plants. They all have strap-shaped fronds, six to eighteen inches long with wavy edges. Some are crested, and some have variegations or markings in varying shades of green. An additional asset to their great charm is their ability to stand even freezing rooms. They must, however, be kept very moist and out of direct sunshine.

PICK-A-BACK PLANT see *Tolmiea menziesii*.

PIGGYBACK PLANT see *Tolmiea menziesii*.

Pilea cadierei ALUMINIUM PLANT, FRIENDSHIP PLANT This decorative, small, bushy plant has pointed, oval leaves that are dark green with broken aluminium stripes. It is easy to grow in an average or warm room, and is excellent for growing in a bottle garden and as a low component of a dish garden. It dislikes strong sunshine and likes plenty of water and liquid manure during the summer. There is a dwarf version, *P. cadierei* 'Nana'.

Pilea microphylla see *Pilea muscosa*.

Pilea muscosa ARTILLERY PLANT, GUNPOWDER PLANT, PISTOL PLANT This plant is quite unlike *P. cadieri* with its minute, light-green, moss-like foliage, but it likes much the same environment. It is

Phyllitis scolopendrium

Above left : Pilea Mollis has decorative corrugated foliage with veins which contrast with the rest of the leaf.

Above right : Another popular variety of Pilea P. Cadierei Nana *is the dwarf version of the commonly grown Aluminium Plant. It too has dark green leaves with broken silvery stripes and is excellent for growing in a bottle garden because of its diminutive size.*

easy to grow. It is also known as *P. microphylla*.

PISTOL PLANT see *Pilea muscosa*.

PITCHER PLANT see *Billbergia*.

Platycerium alcicorne see *Platycerium bifurcatum*.

Platycerium bifurcatum STAGHORN FERN This epiphyte fern is grown on slabs of wood or cork with the roots wrapped in moss and wired in place. They require high humidity and bright light. Spraying the leaves frequently is necessary.

Plectranthus oertendahlii PROSTRATE COLEUS This attractive, trailing plant with leaves that have the principal veins picked out in silver is nearly foolproof for indoor growing. It produces small, rather insignificant, purple flowers. Any part of the stem can be rooted in water.

PORCELAIN FLOWER see *Hoya carnosa*.

PRAYER PLANT see *Maranta leuconeura* 'Kerchoveana'.

Primula This is a very popular flowering pot plant. There are a number of attractive species, all of which have a lengthy flowering season. There is quite a range of colours among the more common ones. *P. kewensis* has small, scented, deep-yellow flowers, those of *P. malacoides* are also small and light purple in colour; *P. obconica* has large rose, blue, red, white or salmon-pink blooms; and those of *P. sinensis* are large and either pink, lilac or white. It should be noted that some people are allergic to *P. obconica*, which can give rise to skin trouble.

Primula

This bizarre plant, Platycerium Alcicorne is an epiphytic fern which naturally grows on the bark of trees without being planted in soil. It can provide an unusual conversation piece since it can be hung simply in a doorway or on a wall.

To be successful, primulas should be placed in a well-lit, draught-free room, away from heat and direct sun. They need plenty of water during flowering. Dead-heading ensures a long succession of brilliantly coloured blooms. They also react well to regular feeding.

Normally primulas are discarded after flowering, but *P. obconica* and *P. sinensis* can be kept from one season to another if they are allowed to stand in a cool, bright room. Illustrated in colour on pages 21 and 44.

Primula kewensis see *Primula*.

Primula malacoides see *Primula*.

Primula obconica see *Primula*.

Primula sinensis see *Primula*.

Pteris argyraea see *Pteris cretica*.

Pteris cretica RIBBON FERN, BRAKE FERN This fairly quick-growing fern is easy to grow in almost any room. Its fronds are divided into segments, as if they have been cut from ribbons of stiff green material. It is a handsome fern for a pot. It does not object to bright light and will prosper on a sunny window-sill. In a very hot position, however, it likes a very moist atmosphere. It needs very good watering during the summer and only slightly less in the winter. *P. cretica*, together with its close relatives, *P. argyraea* and *P. ensiformis* 'Victoriae', which has variegated foliage, are very suitable subjects for bottle gardens.

Pteris ensiformis 'Victoriae' see *Pteris cretica*.

PURPLE HEART see *Setcreasea purpurea*.

Pteris

Rhapis excelsa LADY PALM This palm has fan-shaped, deep-green leaves, which can be kept dark with sulphate of iron. It can stand low temperatures and prefers shade. It produces suckers from the base and in time makes a fine busy clump. It needs fertilizing only once a year and seldom requires re-potting as it grows slowly. Another variety is *R. flabelliformos*.

Rhapis flabelliformos see *Rhapis excelsa*.

Rhoeo discolor BOAT LILY or MOSES IN THE RUSHES This beautiful foliage plant is an interesting example of how popular plant names are derived. Because it has pretty but insignificant blue or white flowers, contained in purple boat or cradle-shaped bracts at the base of its leaves, it has been given its common names. Its real beauty lies in its dark green, long leaves, that are rose-purple underneath. It likes plenty of water, some shade and its leaves sprayed in summer, and a minimum winter temperature of 50°F (10°C). It makes a good tub plant.

Rhoicissus rhomboidea GRAPE IVY This climber and trailer which has much the same glossy, green, veined foliage as *Cissus antarctica*,

Above left : Rhoicissus Rhomboidea *is one of the most popular house plants for beginners as it grows quickly and its shiny dark green leaves make it an attractive plant. Train it to climb on a trellis or use just as effectively in a hanging basket.*

Above right : Although it is the brunt of many jokes, this hardy plant, Sanseviera Trifasciata Laurentii *can withstand much mistreatment. The leaves are slightly twisted and rise almost vertically out of the soil and are mottled with green and grey tinged with yellow. Divide the roots in the spring to increase the number of plants or take leaf cuttings. If you use the latter method the young plant will lack the yellow edges on the leaves.*

Primulas are very pretty and easy-to-grow house plants which can be started from seeds or propagated by division. Place the plants out of direct sunlight in a fairly cool and light position and be careful not to get water on the leaves when watering as this will cause them to turn brown.

can be distinguished from it by the fact that its leaflets emerge from the stem in groups of three at one point, whereas *Cissus antarctica* grow singly at intervals along the stalks. It has very attractive silvery buds and tendrils. It enjoys a centrally-heated room, but is quite tolerant of any average one. It likes good light, but not direct sunshine. It should be watered freely in the summer and moderately in the winter. It is easy to grow, quick-growing, easy to propagate by layering or by cuttings and is probably the most durable of all house plants. It can be kept bushy and compact by pinching out the growing tips of its tallest stems. Older plants produce berries which look like grapes.

RIBBON FERN see *Pteris cretica*.

ROSE BAY see *Nerium oleander*.

Saintpaulia ionantha AFRICAN VIOLET There is little doubt that the African violet is one of the loveliest and most popular of flowering house plants. It is a dainty, low-growing plant that forms clumps of velvety, rounded, fuzzy leaves, that are distinctly veined. The leaves are dark-green and, with some of the many varieties, their undersides are purple. The bright flowers, with their brilliant boss of yellow stamens resemble violets. According to the variety, the colours range from pure white through all shades of pink and mauve to the deepest purple and violet. Saintpaulia stay in flower for several months. African violets are not easy plants to grow, because their demands are exacting, but they can be met by most plant lovers who have centrally-heated rooms and a certain amount of patience. Their first requirement is a temperature that never falls below 60°F (15°C) and is not subject to violent fluctuations. In addition they must have a moist atmosphere, which can be adequately provided by surrounding their pots with moist peat or standing them in a pebble tray. They must have plenty of water, seemingly all the time because they do not appear to have a resting period. Watering should, however, be done from below or with a very narrow-spouted watering can, because they resent having water on their foliage, stalks and their crowns, which will rot if wet. Small plastic pots are best for them, because in clay pots any leaves coming in touch with their rims when they are damp tend to rot. They should not be exposed to draughts or gas fumes. They also appreciate regular doses of liquid feed.

They require good light but not direct sunshine. It has been demonstrated that they require fourteen hours of light every day to be at their best. Fortunately, they are quite happy with artificial light, especially flourescent, so their requirements can be met even on the darkest day by artificially supplementing the daylight.

Although they are quite difficult to grow, they can be easily propagated by planting up root divisions or leaf cuttings in spring.

African violets can produce a spectacular effect when they are planted in bottle gardens and terrariums. They are also delightful as the low-growing components of pot plant arrangements. Illustrated in colour on pages 44-45.

Saxifraga sarmentosa

Sansevieria trifasciata 'Laurentii' MOTHER-IN-LAW'S TONGUE, BAYONET PLANT, SNAKE PLANT This very decorative, but rather vicious-looking plant, is easy to grow. It loves sunshine, but does not mind shade; it is adaptable to high and low temperatures, but at the latter it should be kept fairly dry. It should be allowed to dry out between waterings. It has narrow, fleshy, pointed, slightly twisted leaves, edged with yellow and banded alternatively with light and dark green.

Saxifraga sarmentosa MOTHER OF THOUSANDS or STRAWBERRY GERANIUM This is a low-growing, hardy plant, that likes a cool room and dislikes sunshine. It should be grown in a small pot. Its leaves are particularly decorative and are dark green with cream coloured veins, with their undersides purplish-red. It is easily propagated by layering. Another variety is *S. stolonifera*.

Saxifraga stolonifera see *Saxifraga sarmentosa*.

Schefflera actinophylla UMBRELLA TREE This delightful foliage plant has glossy, green, long pointed leaves in groups of three to seven lobes at the top of a stalk, like the segments of an umbrella. It flourishes in almost any room, even in a dry atmosphere. It grows

Below left : These small plants are related to the ferns and grow quite easily indoors. Selaginellas are dainty and often moss-like in appearance and they grow successfully in a humid, cool and shady position. Do not allow water to settle on the foliage. Take cuttings during spring and summer as they will root very easily then.

Below right : Schefflera actinophylla is a shrubby plant with quite large, glossy green leaves which are divided into three lobes when young and up to seven lobes in older plants. This plant grows quite large and it is possible to raise new plants from cuttings.

Above left : Scindapsus Aureus, *Marble Queen, resembles a variegated philodendron and is an attractive climbing plant with heart-shaped, cream and green speckled leaves. Give it as much light as possible away from direct sunlight during the winter months or else the variegated markings will become less pronounced.*

Above right : Scindapsus Aureus *or Devil's Ivy is a larger leaved variety of the Scindapsus family, and as with philodendrons, the plant will grow better if you insert the aerial roots into the soil of the pot or allow them to cling to a piece of cork bark or a cane covered with moist moss.*

fairly quickly and eventually makes a large plant. The leaves should be sprayed or washed to keep them clean and healthy.

Scindapsus aureus DEVIL'S IVY or JOSEPH'S COAT This plant can quite excusably be mistaken for a variegated philodendron. It does in fact need to be handled in much the same way as these plants. It has heart-shaped, green and yellow leaves. When grown vertically it needs to have the support of a moss stick, so that its numerous aerial roots can absorb moisture. Although it is not so happy grown in this fashion, it is probably one of the best house plants to trail over the edge of a dish garden. It is not an easy plant and does best in slight shade. When it is young the leaves tend to brown at the edge, but if well cared for, this shortcoming is overcome as it becomes established.

Scindapsus aureus 'Marble Queen', which has cream leaves flecked with green, is a somewhat slower grower.

Scindapsus pictus 'Argyraeus', which has silver spotted leaves is also very lovely.

Scolopendrium vulgare see *Phyllitis scolopendrium.*

SCREW PINE see *Pandanus veitchii.*

SEDGE see *Cyperus alternifolius.*

Selaginella CREEPING MOSS These plants are not strictly ferns, but are closely related to them. There are three species which are usually sold by florists. The first is *S. apus*, which has bright-green, prettily shaped leaves; the second is *S. martensii*, with mossy, bright-green foliage, and *S. kraussiana*, which has bright-green, fern-like foliage. With its twelve-inch trailing stems, the latter is an excellent choice for a hanging basket. Perhaps even more lovely is its variety 'Aurea' which has tiny golden leaves.

Selaginellas require damp, shady conditions and moderate warmth, with a winter temperature of about 55°F (13°C).

Selaginella apus see *Selaginella.*

Selaginella kraussiana see *Selaginella.*

Selaginella martensii see *Selaginella.*

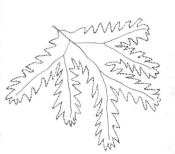

Selaginella

Setcreasea purparea

Senecio cruentus see *Cinerarias*.

Setcreasea purpurea PURPLE HEART This lovely house plant is a quick-grower and an easy plant to cultivate. The lance-shaped leaves are six inches long and about one and three-quarter inches wide, with long, white hairs on their surfaces, which give a fascinating haziness to their purplish green and violet colour. Placed in a good light these tints are intensified and it does not object to sunshine. It will survive during the winter in an unheated room. It makes an attractive member of an arrangement, where it tends to trail over the rim of the container.

SHIELD FERN see *Cyrtomium falcatum*.

SHRIMP PLANT see *Beloperone guttata*.

SILK OAK see *Grevillea robusta*.

Sinningia speciosa see *Gloxinia*.

SLIPPER FLOWER see *Calceolaria*.

SNAKE PLANT see *Sansevieria trifasciata* 'Laurentii'.

SNAKESKIN PLANT see *Fittonia aroyroneura*.

Solanum capsicastrum WINTER CHERRY or CHRISTMAS CHERRY This gay, delightfully coloured shrub, with its pointed, green leaves, and intriguing shiny orange or red berries, brings great cheer to any room, particularly in winter, when it is in great demand. If it is kept in a cool atmosphere, free from draughts, the berries will stay on the bush for months. Great care must be given to watering, because the leaves will fall if the soil dries out completely or becomes waterlogged. Its leaves, flower buds and flowers should be regularly sprayed. Feeding during the time the shrub is berried is advantageous. Fruiting shoots should be cut back to within an inch or two of the main framework after the berries fall.

SOUTH SEA LAUREL see *Codiaeum variegatum pictum*.

Sparmannia africana INDOOR LIME TREE This is a delightful, evergreen pot plant which is hardy. It produces a profusion of attractive, sweet-scented, white flowers from January to May. It likes plenty of water and occasional doses of liquid feed during the

Above left : Solanum capsicastrum *or Winter Cherry produces delicate white flowers with orange centres which are replaced by reddish-orange berries in the winter months. This is an easy and decorative plant to grow and is started from seeds gathered from the berries it produces.*

Above right : The attractive and sweet-scented white flowers of Sparmannia Africana *makes it a delightful pot plant. It is a hardy evergreen named after Dr. A. Sparmann, a botanist who accompanied Captain Cook on his second voyage around the world. It can be placed outdoors in a sunny position during the summer months.*

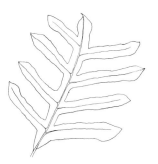

Stenocarpus

Above left : Spathi-
phyllum Wallisii *is an
attractive evergreen
plant with dark green
leaves and white flowers
which resemble those of
the Arum Lily. Propa-
gate by division of the
roots in the spring.*

Above right : Stepha-
notis Floribunda
*produces extremely
beautiful flowers similar
to Jasmine. Its shiny
dark green leaves which
are elongated in shape,
make it an attractive
house plant even when
it is not in bloom.*

summer, with spraying during hot weather. It should be put in a
well-lit spot, out of the draught, and it enjoys spells in the summer
sun. It grows well in an ordinary room, provided the air is not too
dry. It should be kept in shape by pruning after flowering.

Spathiphyllum wallisii PEACE LILY This plant grows into a clump of
slim, pointed leaves on fairly long stems. Its flowers are typical of
the spathes of an arum lily, but smaller, and in colour are first light
green, then white and finally green. They are very elegant and last
about a month. It is easy to grow in a warm, shady position with
good humidity. It delights in central heating and does not object to
deep shade, but loathes bright sunlight which turns its foliage
yellow.

Spathiphyllum wallisii 'Mauna Loa' is a larger version of *S. wallisii*.
SPIDER PLANT see *Chlorophytum capense* 'Variegatum'.
SPIRAEA see *Astilbe*.
STAG'S HORN FERN see *Platycerium bifurcatum*.
STARFISH PLANT see *Cryptanthus*.
STAR OF BETHLEHEM see *Campanula isophylla*.
STAR PLANT see *Cryptanthus*.

Stenocarpus sinuatus is another easy-to-grow, nearly hardy plant,
that is suitable for cold and average rooms, which are well lit. It
does not like direct sunshine. It is very decorative, with light-green,
glossy leaves that have a slight wave. The young leaves have three
lobes, but they increase in number with age. With its leaves growing to six inches long, it can ultimately become large.

Stephanotis floribunda MADAGASCAR JASMINE This plant is an exotic-
looking, highly perfumed, vigorous climber. Its blooms are similar
to *Jasminium polyanthum*.

The waxen, white flowers have a rich scent, which can be overpowering in a small room. They grow in clusters or bunches along
the length of its stems, which need supporting. It has evergreen
leaves that are about three inches long and make an excellent foil
to the blooms. It should be kept fairly warm, and never below 55°F

(13°C) during winter, with its pot surrounded by damp peat and occasionally sprayed to maintain the humidity. Illustrated in colour on pages 22 and 46.

SWEETHEART VINE see *Philodendron scandens*.

SWISS CHEESE PLANT see *Monstera deliciosa*.

SWORD FERN see *Nephrolepsis exaltata*.

Syngonium podophyllum GOOSE FOOT This most attractive plant, with its three-pronged, arrowhead-like, cream-tinted leaves, and many aerial roots, thrives most happily when climbing a moist moss stick. It grows pretty well in warm or average rooms, under normal household conditions. The pot should be allowed to dry out between waterings. Its near relative, *S. vellozianum*, grows satisfactorily in a fairly shady place. An attractive variety is *S. podophyllum* 'Emerald Gold'.

Syngonium podophyllum 'Emerald Gold' see *Syngonium podophyllum*.

Syngonium vellozianum see *Syngonium podophyllum*.

Tetrastigma voinierianum CHESTNUT VINE or LIZARD PLANT This plant derives its name from its dark-green, horse chestnut-shaped leaves, which can measure almost a foot across. It is a fairly large, quick-growing, climbing plant and requires plenty of room, which makes it very suitable for large offices, vestibules and shops. It likes good, even light, but not direct sunlight, a large pot, to be well watered in the summer, with infrequent watering in the winter, to be fed regularly in the summer, moist air and warmth.

Thunbergia alata BLACK-EYED-SUSAN This lovely plant bears open, orange-yellow, black-centred flowers on trailing stems. It does best in light airy positions, and looks well in hanging baskets or cascading from window boxes. Normal room temperature, plenty of water throughout the growing season and fortnightly feeding will keep it happy. Raise new plants from seeds each spring and pot singly in small pots. Nip out growing tip to make plant branch and

Above left : Syngonium makes a good hanging or climbing plant and is not difficult to grow. It has two common varieties, S. podophyllum *which has triangular, green leaves and which produces aerial roots and* S. vellozianum *with dark green leathery leaves with three lobes which makes rather small aerial roots.*

Above right : This amusing plant Tolmiea is commonly called The Piggyback Plant. *It has hairy, heart-shaped green leaves on which little plantlets appear which can be potted up into small pots. It grows into a low, bushy shape which is very pleasing.*

form several flowering shoots. Discard the plant after flowering.

Tolmiea menziesii PICK-A-BACK PLANT, PIGGYBACK PLANT This hardy, ground-covering creeper is easy to grow, and grows in cold and average rooms. It likes shade and plenty of water and regular feeding during the summer, with reduced watering in the winter. It freely grows plantlets on its leaves that can be cut off and potted.

TOTEM POLE PHILODENDRON see *Philodendron cordatum*.

Tradescantia albiflora This plant has leaves with green, pink and white markings, and is a species suitable for hanging baskets. Its cultivar, 'Tricolor', is also very lovely.

Tradescantia albiflora 'Tricolor' see *Tradescantia albiflora*.

Tradescantia blossfeldiana This variety, which has green, glossy leaves that are purple underneath, is a little more difficult to grow.

Tradescantia fluminensis 'Aurea' see *Tradescantia fluminensis*.

Tradescantia fluminensis WANDERING JEW, TRAVELLING SAILOR or WANDERING PLANT This type is the best known of the species. There are both yellow and white variegated forms as well as green. If the former revert to green, such shoots should be cut off immediately. They are easy to grow in average and warm rooms if given plenty of water in the summer and considerably less in the winter, and good light. They will grow in shade, but they lose a good deal of their beautiful colour. Most tradescantias become straggly and defoliated with age, particularly in a dry atmosphere. They are so easily propagated from cuttings that this can be readily overcome by replacing them from time to time. They are most useful house plants for wall brackets, hanging baskets, trailing over the edge of containers and in bottle gardens. Attractive varieties of *T. fluminensis* are 'Variegata' with white stripes on green leaves and 'Aurea' with yellow stripes.

Tradescantia fluminensis 'Variegata' see *Tradescantia fluminensis*.

Tradescantia zebrina see *Zebrina pendula*.

TRAVELLING SAILOR see *Tradescantia fluminensis*.

UMBRELLA PLANT see *Cyperus alterni folius* and *Schefflera actinophylla*.

URN PLANT see *Aechmea*.

Below left : Thunbergia alata, Black-eyed-Susan, is also well known as a garden annual and is attractive and easy to grow inside or out. It flowers from June to September.

Below right : Tradescantias make very attractive hanging plants which prefer a well-lit position away from direct sun. Propagation is very simple as cuttings root easily. Pinch out the growing tips of the plant to prevent them from becoming too scraggly and to encourage bushy growth.

Thunbergia

VARIEGATED PINEAPPLE see *Ananas comosum* 'Variegatus'.
VELVET PURPLE PLANT see *Gynura*.
Vriesia splendens PAINTED FEATHERS This is another beautiful and spectacular bromeliad. Its large, strap-like leaves, that are banded brown and soft green in colour and dark reddish brown on the reverse, form a funnel-shaped rosette with a central vase, which is kept filled with water. From this base there emerges a flower spike, which bears at its top a bright scarlet, spear-shaped bract, which might be at least two feet long. Although it tolerates a dark corner, it prefers to stand in good light. It should have a winter temperature of not less than 55°F (13°C).

Vriesia splendens

WANDERING JEW see *Tradescantia fluminensis*.
WANDERING PLANT see *Tradescantia fluminensis*.
WATERMELON PEPEROMIA see *Peperomia sandersii*.
WAX PLANT see *Hoya Carnosa*.
WEEPING FIG see *Ficus benjamina*.
WHITMAN FERN see *Nephrolepsis exaltata bostoniensis*.
WILLOW FIG see *Ficus benjamina*.
WINTER CHERRY see *Solanum capsicastrum*.
WOOD SORRELL see *Oxalis*.

ZEBRA PLANT see *Aphelandra squarrosa* 'Loisisae'.
Zebrina pendula This plant which is closely related to the tradescantias, is a very beautiful, easily grown plant that can be used for much the same purposes. The upper surfaces of its leaves are silvery, edged green, with a purple centre stripe and bright purple on their undersides, which colours are appreciably enhanced if the plant is kept a little on the dry side. *Z. purpusii* has dark-mauve, rather large leaves.
Zebrino purpusii see *Zebrina pendula*.

Right : Thunbergia grandiflora *is a beautiful evergreen climber which has clusters of pale blue flowers from June to September. The ideal conditions are found in a large greenhouse.*

The Zebrina Pendula *is another easily grown hanging plant which is similar to the Tradescantias. The leaves of this plant are bigger and are striped with silver and green above with purple undersides and it needs good light to maintain the colours. Cuttings root easily in water.*

Bulbs

Nothing brings greater joy than to have spring flowers flourishing in the house during wintertime. Some people have difficulty growing bulbs indoors, but if a few basic rules are followed and the bulbs are obtained from a reliable source the results should be most satisfactory.

You can buy bulbs from your usual dealer or from department stores or you can choose them from catalogues supplied by nurseries and seed companies. If you are choosing bulbs yourself, pick healthy looking ones which are large, plump and firm. Bulbs that will bloom in mid-winter have been specially cultivated and stored under controlled conditions of humidity and temperature. The bulb contains in embryo the already formed leaves, stem and flower and all that has to be done is to provide the right conditions for it to grow and blossom.

There are several methods of indoor cultivation. Hyacinths and crocuses, for instance, can be grown in specially designed bulb glasses which have a shelf in the upper portion on which the bulb can rest. The lower section is filled with water containing a few pieces of charcoal (to keep the water sweet) so that the water just touches the bottom of the bulb. It is then kept in the dark for about eight weeks by which time the roots will have formed. At this time, the water level is lowered so that there is an air space between the water and the bottom of the bulb. This prevents the bulb from rotting. The glass is then placed in semi-shade for a few days before being moved into a lighter position.

Bunch-flowered narcissi can be grown on pebbles in water. In early autumn fill a bowl with pebbles to just two inches below the rim. The bulbs are stood and supported on this with more pebbles and the bowl is then nearly filled with stones. Water, preferably rainwater, containing a little charcoal is put in to a level just below the bottom of the bulbs. Place the bowl in a cool place for about six months. It can be stood in either a dark or light position. After this time, the plants should be given an airy place on a window-sill at a steady temperature of 50-55°F (10-13°C). They should not be stood near a radiator. By mid-winter the narcissi should bloom and continue to do so for quite a while.

The most usual way of planting bulbs indoors is in bowls or other containers. If the bulb is being grown for flowering once indoors and then to be planted out in the garden, a special bulb fibre based on peat, with charcoal and crushed shell added to keep the mixture sweet, is the best type of medium to use. These bulbs may be grown in pots with or without draining holes. Watering is more tricky in bowls without drainage. It is necessary to water regularly to keep the peat fibre moist but be sure there is no excess water left in the bottom of the bowl. Excess water can be tipped

Left : The stately Amaryllis is a hybrid developed from a species native to South America. The stalks, which bear the pale pink flowers tinged with mauve, reach a height of two feet in September to October when the plant flowers. Later the strap-like leaves appear, with the trumpet-shaped flowers growing in bunches of two to four on a stem. Amaryllis bulbs are very large and are planted so that they are only half-buried in the soil. Support the plant with stakes as the weight of the flowers may make it top heavy.

a

b

c

d

out, gently holding the bulbs and fibres in place.

Bulbs such as those of Hippeastrums which are to be grown in the same pot for years need to be potted originally in a fairly good, loam-based, potting soil. If this is not available, one of the peat-based mixtures may be used.

When planting bulbs, the depth at which they should be planted is important. A good guide for hyacinths, daffodils and narcissi is to have their noses just visible, for tulips to be just covered and for small bulbs to have their tips quarter to half inch below the surface.

Although there may be some variation depending on the type of bulb, there is a standard procedure which is likely to be successful for most bulbs. Moisten the bulb fibre before use by putting it in a bucket and pouring over water allowing it to soak for a few hours. Put a layer of charcoal in the bottom of the bowl and put a layer of fibre on top of the charcoal after squeezing out the excess moisture. Press the fibre down gently. If you make it too firm the roots of the bulb will find it difficult to work their way down into the fibre and may just push against it and lift the bulb out of the bowl. Most bulbs are set between three and four inches deep and should be

a

b

c

d

e

f

planted so that after they have been set on the layer of bulb fibre, more fibre can be added around them so that they are adequately covered, with half inch left between the top of the bulb fibre and the rim of the bowl to allow for watering.

The bulbs usually provide the best display when planted closely together – just make sure they are not touching each other or the sides of the bowl. As you will want all the bulbs in one bowl to produce blooms at the same time, only plant one type of bulb in a bowl.

Once the bulbs have been planted the bowl is then 'plunged', that is, placed in a cool dark place for eight to ten weeks. Treating the bulbs in this way will encourage an adequate root system to form before too much top growth is produced. The bulbs can be placed in a cool, shady place in the garden and covered with a few inches of moist, not wet peat, sand or soil. If it proves to be an exceptionally dry period, watering may be necessary because the bowls must not be allowed to dry out.

A neater way of plunging the bowls is to make a wooden box of suitable size into which the bowls are placed and covered with sand or similar material. In either of these methods, the bowl of bulbs should be first put in a well-perforated, plastic bag or wrapped in newspaper to keep the fibre clean. Those who have no garden can place the bowls in a cool, dark cupboard or cellar or on a balcony. If there is no alternative, the container can be kept in a dark corner covered with an overturned cardboard box or black plastic bag.

After the appropriate time, the blanched top growth should be about one to two inches high. The bowls are then placed in a shady position in a cool room where they can become accustomed to daylight. The growth will green and after about a week the bulbs can be moved to a warm, sunny spot where they are intended to flower.

Below : Nerine sarneinsis *is the most beautiful species of the Nerine family. It produces large bunches of iridescent flowers on stems which grow up to two feet high, and many varieties have been raised with flowers varying from pure white through shades of pale pink and orange scarlet to magenta. Its popular name of Guernsey Lily derives from bulbs shipwrecked on the coast of the island which began to grow in the sand along the shore, and the plants are hardy outside in the Channel Islands. Its bulbs are large and shaped rather like that of the narcissus with several papery layers encasing the bulb itself.*

Top right : The spectacular flowers of Amaryllis Hippeastrum make it a much prized bulb to grow indoors. Blooming in early autumn, these plants provide dramatic splashes of colour.

Below left : Hyacinth 'Jan Bos' is an early flowering variety of florists' hyacinths which has been derived from H. orientalis through a long process of crossbreeding and selection resulting in larger and stouter plants. These bulbs are suitable for forcing indoors so that they bloom in winter and early spring.

Below right : Narcissus is a vast genus including species flowering from autumn until late spring. Some of these varieties have been developed so as to be suitable for forcing indoors, for example Narcissus Barrett Browning.

Water the bowls frequently to prevent the fibre from drying out, but do not overwater. Continue this procedure freely all the time they are in flower.

Some flowers such as narcissi need supports. Four thin stakes or canes can be inserted around the sides of the bowl and joined with raffia to keep the plants upright and stop them from drooping as they grow.

Once the flowers have died, remove them but continue to water the bulbs until the leaves turn yellow and die down. They can then be dried off and kept in a dry cool place ready for planting in the garden in September. They will take two to three years to recover from being forced indoors. Narcissi grown in water should be thrown away as they are never much good after this treatment.

The following list of annual bulbs can be grown successfully indoors following this method: daffodils, crocuses, hyacinths, snowdrops, tulips and narcissi. The most common type of permanent bulbs which will last from year to year is the Amaryllis.

To start these bulbs growing, the roots and lower parts are soaked in lukewarm water for several days. Sufficient compost composed of good loam and leaf mould plus a little silver sand is placed in the container to form a cone on which the bulb is stood with its roots spread out. The cone should be high enough so that when the planting is completed, the bulb stands half-way out of the soil. Give the pot bottom heat to encourage development by placing it on a warm mantlepiece or radiator shelf. When the buds are formed, it should be transferred to a sunny window-sill. For a fortnight after, watering should be sparse and it should be given tepid water from the top, *never from the bottom*.

After flowering, the plant should be put in a cool place. It should be given water while it grows, but once it has stopped, the watering should be gradually diminished to almost nothing during the winter. It should then be put in a cool, frost-free place.

Below : Like many other spring flowering shrubs, crocuses grow in water anchored by stones or pebbles. A little charcoal added to the stones keeps the water sweet. Crocuses are best kept in a cold place until the flower buds show when you can bring them into a warm room.

Right : Old-fashioned double daffodils lack the charm of the single varieties but are useful for making a strong effect planted in pots of soil. The tall 'Harvest Gold' daffodils are growing in fibre. Double tulips, scillas, grape hyacinths and hyacinths will all flower at the same time to create a lovely display of spring flowers complemented by the colours of a cineraria.

Opposite top left :
Vallota speciosa *is a beautiful permanent bulb plant, popularly known as the Scarborough Lily, which produces heads of funnel-shaped red-toned flowers in late summer. The foliage is evergreen which makes it a most attractive plant to grow indoors and it can remain in the same pot for two or three years.*

Opposite top right :
Nerine 'Brian Doe' *produces usually large heads of satin-pink flowers. Replant nerines in pots every fourth or fifth year since the bulbs increase freely by division, and do any repotting in August or early September before flower spikes form.*

Left : A grouping of pots of different varieties of narcissus creates a lovely display of spring colour on a window sill. Some cactus plants stood in the foreground balance the height of the narcissi and add a contrast of texture and shape to the composition.

Above left : A dish of early flowering tulips such as this scarlet display of T. eichleri *makes winter seem much shorter. Planted close together in a dish, the plants support each other and produce a cheerful mass of colour.*

Above right : This mixed group of Narcissus flowers shows the extent of the variety in colour and shape of this large family.

Left : A display of various sorts of bulbs which can be forced indoors includes crocuses, scillas and tulips as well as hyacinths grown either in bulb fibre or in the specially designed glass jars in which the bulb rests on a ledge with the roots extending into the water. Sprinkle a little grass seed over the surface of the pot to make a nice bed from which the plant stalk can grow.

Cacti & Succulents

Cacti and succulents include some of the most beautiful and some of the most bizarre plants. They offer great enjoyment and interest and at the same time are easier to care for than most other house plants. These plants are native to the Americas and Africa, from the sub-zero areas of Canada and the hot, arid deserts of Mexico to the humid rain forests of South America.

All cacti are succulents, but not all succulents are cacti. The main characteristic of a succulent is the fact that it has either an extremely fleshy stem or very fleshy leaves or both. The chief function of the fleshy foliage is that it is able to hold moisture during the long and very hot periods of sun. A plant that has to grow in an open, dry situation must be constructed in this way. Most succulents grow directly in sand or soil, but some 'squat' on other plants, usually trees. These are not parasites as they get the nourishment they need from the air.

The true cacti belong to the family Cactaceae and have fleshy water-retaining stems but no leaves. Cacti usually have spines and they all have aureoles which look like little pincushions. It is from these aureoles that the spines or hairs grow, as well as the flowers and offsets.

In order to reach water, some plants will send down their roots very deep. On the other hand, many species have very shallow fibrous roots so they are able to absorb the evening dew quickly. Some succulents may look totally dried up and shrunken during their resting period, that is to say during the months when they receive no water. Others take the precaution of bearing their leaves in a rosette form which can close up in the hottest sun and thereby reduce transpiration as well as giving protection.

The strong spines on many species of cactus help to protect the plants from feeding animals. They also help to deflect the sun's rays. They encourage the collection of moisture and also provide shade. This is particularly the case with very hairy plants. Some succulents have stems similar to some true cacti, for instance, varieties of the *Stapelia* genus. This genus produces starfish-like flowers whose smell attracts flies thus ensuring pollination.

When plants live normally in tropical conditions or in arid areas, they undergo particularly dramatic climactic changes. They may be baked almost dry for months at a time and then deluged with torrential rains. The result is that during the dry periods the plant grows very little and during the torrents it not only does most of its growing, but it produces flowers and fruit as well.

Revelling in good light, this particular leaf-flowering cactus, Schlumbergera gaertneri *blooms in spring, hence its popular name, the Easter Cactus. The cascades of colour produced by this type of cactus make it especially appropriate for a festive season. Other hybrids bloom at Christmas and their flowers cover a range of colour from white to pinks and reds.*

Right : Mammallaria wildii *is a member of the largest single genus of cacti, and is especially suitable for the beginner to grow as it is quite tough.* M. wildii *is a quick growing variety which produces attractive rings of whitish pink flowers amidst its profusion of spiny rosettes.*

Below : Parodia microsperma *with its long hooked spines produces flowers which range from red to yellow. As long as they are not over-potted, Parodias will grow and flower well, blooming through the whole summer.*

Right : Epiphyllum ackermannii *is a leaf cactus which forms a bushy plant with wavy, notched leaves. The spines are present round the narrower stems and only in the notches in the stem when the plants are young. The flowers are most often red, but some varieties of leaf cactus produce orange or white flowers.*

Below right : Aporocactus flagelliformis, *commonly called the Rat's Tail Cactus, is a very popular cactus with its hanging green spiny stems and abundantly produced magenta flowers. Take care to prevent the stems from rotting back.*

Left : Opuntia microdasys *or Prickly Pear Cactus is a popular cactus and is easy to grow. This variety forms an erect and spreading bush and is covered with prickly aureoles*

Above : Astrophytums *or Bishop's Cap Cacti are becoming more and more popular.* Astrophytum myriostigma *flowers quite easily and has an attractive flecked body and no spines.*

Right : Echinopsis eyriesii *is a globular cactus producing many offsets. Its flowers are borne at the end of a tube from the side of the plant.*

Below : Stapelias *are succulents which are pollinated by blow flies and in order to attract them, the flowers give off a strong and unpleasant smell.* Stapelia variegata *is the most common species and produces yellow flowers covered with dark brown flecks.*

Left : Crown of Thorns or Euphorbia splendens *is a member of a large family of succulents which include the poinsettia. Its stems are stiff and spiney, and it bears red flowers in pairs at the ends of the branches.*

Above left : Chamacereus silvestrii *commonly called The Peanut Cactus grows well and produces attractive orange flowers.*

Above right : Kalanchoe blossfeldiana *is a dwarf shrubby succulent which grows in clumps. Its thick green stem is almost obscured by the oval, green leaves which grow opposite each other on the short stalks, and the flowers, which grow in dense bunches, are most commonly red.*

Below left : Echeveria levcotricha *is a small succulent shrub lightly covered with white hairs. Its boat-shaped leaves are tinged with brownish red toward the point, and it bears bright red flowers on stems at the sides of the rosettes.*

Below right : Conophytum pearsonii *is commonly called Pebble Plant or Living Stone because of the shape of its clumps of rounded stems. It produces a profusion of flowers during September and October although during its resting period in the summer the plant looks like a stone while the outer skin dies off and nourishment is transferred to the fresh young plant growing below.*

Overleaf : *Cacti make attractive and interesting dish gardens which are well-suited for life in an office.*

It is not only that cacti and succulents are fascinating plants, they can be very decorative as well. They all produce flowers and sometimes quite dramatic and showy ones.

The flower colours in cacti vary from dark crimson to violet, from orange to pink and red and from yellow to white. Most of the flowers have a delicate metallic sheen. Many of the finest blooms open at night. The flowers open in their full glory when the sun sets and are at their best at midnight and have faded by dawn. Other cacti produce flowers which last for a day or two. Some have longer-lasting flowers which open during the day and close at night. A few like those of the *Echinopsis* are beautifully perfumed.

There are plants which bloom every season or even several times in one season even under what are not ideal conditions. It is important to follow some rules, however, to encourage flowering. The plants must be allowed to rest for several months a year with the temperature never dropping below 40°F (5°C). Always see that the plants have plenty of fresh air. The plants should be watered quite freely in the summer with the amounts being reduced in autumn.

When buying succulents it always makes sense to go to a reliable nurseryman and tell him that you want plants that will flower. Be sure to buy plants that have not been grown too rapidly. If the cactus plant has been forced by giving it too much water and heat it is not likely to flower and is likely to die in household conditions.

The flowers are followed by fruit which is usually one-celled berries. Some of the plants produce fruit which is edible. The fruit of the Prickly Pear or *Opuntia microdasys*, is particularly refreshing especially if you get someone else to peel it for you. The fruit is covered with very fine hairy spines and when these get into the skin they can be very uncomfortable.

The red fruits of some of the *Mammillaria* cacti have a strawberry-like flavour. Mexicans eat berries shaped very much like olives picked from a species of *Myrtillocactus*. In tropical countries, some of the *Opuntias* are used as green fodder for cattle. The

Above left : A cultivar of Epiphyllum *shows the size of the flowers produced in proportion to the size of the plant. Plants are inclined to produce more buds than flowers so bud drop is normal. Nature permits only as many buds to mature as the plant can support.*

Opposite top left : Epiphyllum oxypetalum, *often called Orchid Cactus, is the most commonly grown of night-flowering cactus which produces giant white blooms almost ten inches across giving off a heavy fragrance.*

Opposite top right : Cephalocereus senilis *or Old Man Cactus is slow growing and difficult to make flower. It is covered with long flowing white hair-like bristles and has small blooms which are white and nocturnal.*

Left : A dish planted with Chamaecereus silvestrii *makes an attractive dish garden and is a good species for the beginner to grow, as it requires little care and grows quite quickly producing flowers freely.*

Above right : This miniature variety of Rebutia, R. kesselringiana *is a tiny globe cactus which blooms in a halo of colour. As it is so small it can be used effectively in miniature gardens.*

outside is scorched in an open fire in order to burn off the spines.

There is a type of Mexican *Agave* from which is made a very popular alcoholic drink called Pulque and there are species of *Aloes* which contain resins that can be used medicinally. One type of *Euphorbia* produces gum used by veterinary surgeons and other varieties are used as hedging plants because of their thorns. These thorns are used as sewing needles in Mexico and elsewhere. As you can see, these plants are useful as well as decorative.

Although many house plants require high humidity and frequent watering, most cacti and succulents can, if necessary endure a drought and need only average home humidity. With good light and weekly watering, most grow unattended for months. And they will survive even if we forget to water them for a time. Light and soil are of vital importance to cacti and succulents. The medium in which they are planted must drain readily yet still supply an adequate amount of moisture to the plants. Cacti and succulents like plenty of light and like to grow in a place where there is plenty of reflected light. They prefer rooms where the walls are light or even white rather than dark walls.

The South American cacti which are often called globe cacti need bright and airy situations where there is some sunlight. There are some exceptions – rebutias and lobivias – that will tolerate partial shade, but sunlight will produce a more beautiful crop of flowers.

Keep globe cacti on the dry side from November to February. In most regions, this resting period coincides with cold weather. Do not try to force the plants but wait until the first signs of growth in spring and then start watering sparingly as the warm weather approaches.

Turn the plants occasionally so that light reaches all parts of the plant. Do not turn them when they are in bud as the change of light can cause the buds to drop.

Succulents other than cacti vary in light requirements. Echeverias need almost full sun and kalanchoes such as *Kalanchoe blossfeldiana* and *K. pumila* do better in light shade. Most sedums grow well in full sun but a few are shade tolerant.

There are many different soils for cacti and succulents. They do not grow in pure sand as is sometimes supposed but require a good nutritional soil. Commercial potting soil mixed with some vermiculite and sharp sand to ensure good drainage provides an ideal medium.

Because they grow so slowly, cacti and other succulents need transplanting only infrequently. As a simple rule, transplanting should take place annually in the case of plants which have grown larger than a fist. If they are smaller, they do not need to be transplanted more often than every three or four years. Really large specimens are not transplanted at all, but some soil is taken away and replaced with fresh compost every five years or so.

It is a good idea to leave young seedlings in their boxes or pans for two years. They do well in company and after this time they can be potted up separately. Even then, the pots can be stood quite close together to maintain this bond. Young plants require a change of soil every two years. It is important to be sure that there is room in the pot for the roots and that there is nutriment in the soil to feed the plant.

The best time to transplant is in the spring when the plant is starting growth again. It is a good idea to have clean clay pots which can be sterilized by being stood in boiling water for ten minutes or so. Plastic pots can be cleaned with a medium formaldehyde solution such as is used for de-scaling kettles.

Take the plant that is to be re-potted, invert it and knock it out of its pot. Remove the crocks at the base of the plant and tease out the roots a little at the base while looking for insect pests which sometimes attack the roots. If these are present, treat with a commercial pest killer.

Start to remove the old compost with a pair of tweezers being careful not to damage the roots. If you find areas of root which are matted together and dead, these may be cut out. If any roots are broken during this operation, trim them with a razor so that it is a clean cut. A light dusting of powder hormone on any damaged roots will prevent any effect to the plant.

Once the majority of old soil is removed, pick a pot one size larger than the original one in which to pot the plant. Put plenty of crocks in the bottom of the new pot to the depth of one inch. Put a layer of peat on top and add some compost. Hold the plant in the middle of the pot so that the roots are spread out and fill around it with compost turning the pot from time to time to make sure the soil is even all around.

Don't make the compost too firm as it will settle down later on. Leave about a half an inch at the top for watering. Be sure that the plant is planted at the same depth as it was before. The potting soil should be just moist so that no further water is needed for a fortnight. New root hairs will develop in the warm, moist compost and the addition of new water during this period would not only cool

Below left : Crassula lycopodoides, *a strange rose-like plant which produces minute yellow flowers in the axils of its dense leaves, grows in a branched formation like heather and is seldom more than six inches high. The very small dark green leaves are arranged in four rows around the stem giving it a square appearance.*

Below right : The Golden Barrel, or Grandmother's Armchair Cactus, Echinocactus grusonii *is useful in small collections. This type of cactus seldom flowers, but produces a certain amount of wool on top as it gets old.*

Aporocactus is a genus of cacti that are members of the Cereus family and have slender, creeping or pendulous stems often branching with areole roots. The flowers are tubular and turn up from the stems of the plant.

down the soil but would also fill up some of the vital air spaces.

Start your collection of cacti and succulents with mature plants and do not buy too many. After you have succeeded with half a dozen, you can add to your collection, confident that the plants will respond to the conditions your home provides.

Eventually you will want to try to have a variety of cacti and succulents with different characteristics and which produce flowers of varying colours. Every collection should try to obtain a plant of *Pereskia* of some sort and no collection would be complete without some of the Prickly Pear cacti of the *Opuntia* genus.

The upright and columnar cacti come in several types. *Stetsonia coryne* has attractive black spines but is slow growing and *Oreocereus celsainus* has attractive woolly hairs almost completely covering its brown spines. *Cleistocactus straussii* is a good ornament in any collection with its sleeky white hairs. The Old Man Cactus, *Cephalocereus senilis* is popular and interesting, but it too is very slow growing.

The Rat's Tail Cactus, *Aporocactus flagelliformis* is also popular with its hanging green stems and abundant red flowers. The Peanut Cactus, *Chamaecereus silvestrii* is a good grower and produces attractive orange flowers. Every collection must include a representative of the genus *Lobivia*. We recommend *Lobivia famatimensis* which is easy to flower and which comes in a large variety of colours. *Rebutias* are essential cacti especially as they are the easiest to flower. *Rebutia minuscula* produces red flowers, *R. marsoneri* has yellow blooms and *R. violaciflora* has lilac flowers.

Matucana aurantiaca which is a member of the Echinocactanae family, characterized by the way the flower buds unfold with the

Top left : Echeveria
retusa hybrida *is a
shrubby succulent with
glaucous grey-green
leaves rounded at the
tops. It produces flowers
in rosettes at the ends of
the branches.*

Bottom left : Echeveria
graptopalum weinbergii
is another variety of
Echeveria *which forms
low-growing rosettes
seldom exceeding two
inches in height. The
fleshy leaves are rounded
and end in a point, and
its flowers are borne on*

spines from the growing point at the top of the plant, is a plant every beginner should try. It produces showy orange flowers which are tubular in shape.

Representatives of the *Parodia* genus which grow and flower well, and of the *Notocactus* genus should be included in the selection, as well as *Ferocacti* with their vicious spines, *Echinofossulocacti* with their deeply divided wrinkled ribs and mammalliarias. A good collection is rounded out by Leaf Cacti, like the familiar Christmas Cactus, *Zygocactus truncatus* and the Whitsun Cactus, *Schlumbergera gaertneri.* These lovely plants produce an abundance of flowers and enhance any collection.

Other succulents which are of interest are the aeoniums and the aloes. The Partridge-breasted Aloe, *Aloe variegata* appreciates more shades than most succulents.

Many members of the *Conophytum* and *Crassula* genuses make excellent succulents to include in a collection. *Crassula aborescens*

*slender stems rising from
the rosettes.*

Top right : Crassula
lactea *the Jade Plant,
makes an excellent pot
plant as it endures wind,
shade, drought and even
too much water. It is the
largest growing Crassula, often reaching
eight to ten feet in height
and its flowers are
racemes of pale pink
blossoms.*

Bottom right : The Aloe
variegata *or Partridge*

is a fine dwarf shrub that makes an attractive 'tree' in a pot. Echeverias too make good plants to start with like *Echeveria derenbergii*
and *E. gibbiflora*. The euphorbias are one of the largest succulent
families and a good collection is sure to contain several varieties.
These include the popular Crown of Thorns, *Euphorbia splendens*
and the familiar Poinsettia *E. pulcherrima*.

Haworthias are good plants for beginners to try since they flower
easily as do some hoyas. Kalanchoes ranging from the Tom Thumb
varieties to the larger *Kalanchoe beharensis* is a popular family
which includes Mother of Thousands, *K. daigremontiana*. Lithops
which are commonly called Living Pebbles are a curious form of
succulent, which resemble smooth stones.

The types of cacti and succulents are endless. Once you develop
an interest in them and show that you can provide them with a
happy home, they will provide hours of fascination as well as
decorative accents in your home.

Dish &
Bottle Gardens

Single plants are effective decoration in a room so long as there are not too many and they are arranged in some way. However, if it is not desirable to create a display, or if the space available is limited, this is often done better by grouping several plants in one container.

It is essential that the plants chosen to live together in one container enjoy the same conditions as it will not be possible to vary the environment to suit incompatible or fussy plants. If this rule is not followed, the arrangement is destined to fail from the start. This restriction will not present much of a limitation, however, as there are innumerable plants which will enjoy each other's company and which will flourish in the same atmospheric conditions.

The most attractive arrangements of houseplants in a container are composed of plants varying in height and in growing habit which have contrasts in foliage shapes and colours. Combining plants in this way will create a pleasing composition both in shape and colour. A typical well-proportioned grouping should contain one predominantly tall plant with several bushy ones of varying low heights to act as a foil, and one or two trailing plants to overhang the container or creep on the surface.

There are two general methods for planting several house plants together in the same container. The first method is simply a matter of knocking the individual plants out of their pots and planting them together in compost in the normal way, arranging them as desired. It is important to ensure that there is good drainage in the container in which they are planted.

The alternative method is to put a layer of moist peat into the container and to stand the individual pots on this. This is perhaps more properly called 'plant arranging'. The pots are then packed round with more damp peat up to the rims of the pots. This method has the advantage that plants liking different soil types but the same environmental conditions can be grouped in the same container. It also makes it possible to give the plants different levels of watering and allows pot plants and bulbs to be included, giving the grouping colour at varying times of the year. Plants can be positioned at an angle if the arrangement demands it. Generally, the plant arrangement is more easily altered with this method.

It is possible to use both these methods of planting in the same container to achieve the maximum effect from the types of plants used.

Dish gardens can also be made with cuttings of all kinds, stem, leaf, offsets and stolons in such a way that they will root in the container, or rooted cuttings can be used for this purpose. This is a simple and effective way of growing little plants and a good way of using any tips you may think it best to nip out from a vigorous, mature plant. This type of gardening is also an ideal way to learn

A dish garden containing a blooming cyclamen, variegated peperomia and climbing ivy among other foliage plants is a lovely centrepiece for a table.

about propagating plants and growing in general. It is most satisfying to plant small shoots and offcuts in an arrangement and to watch it flourish into an attractive dish garden.

Bottle gardens which will be dealt with in detail later, demand some skill to plant, but this is a very absorbing and rewarding task. Magnificent arrangements can be grown in a variety of glass bottles and the effect of these gardens under glass is always quite dramatic. Once the plants have grown, the arrangement presents the familiar puzzle of the ship in the bottle which adds to their charm.

There is a multitude of containers suitable for creating a dish garden in all sorts of shapes and made in a variety of materials. The most common are, of course, made of porcelain, earthenware, glass or plastic. The container in which the plants are arranged should be chosen carefully so that the shape and colour of the container add to the overall effect of the composition. Some of the

This miniature garden in a dish includes a tiny bush and a miniature variety of heather which adds colour to a selection of foliage plants. The stones create the atmosphere of a full-sized garden to this tiny environment.

Above left : This well-planned dish garden includes tall plants in the back of the arrangement which act as a foil for the lower growing varieties planted in the front. Two sorts of trailing plant are included to drape decoratively over the edge of the container.

Above right : In this dish garden arrangement, the contrast in the size of leaves is an important factor. The delicate fronds of the palm contrast with the large broad ivy leaves and the flat foliage of the fern, with African violet blooms adding a touch of colour to the garden.

newer plastic containers are made in unfortunate colours and a coat of neutral paint will often vastly improve the look of the vessel. Dish gardens can be planted in a variety of improvised containers as well, such as sea shells, tea pots which have lost their lids and sauce boats. Baskets make very effective containers for dish gardens once they are fitted with suitable damp-proof interiors. Small laundry baskets, work baskets and even outgrown dog baskets can be used to contain a garden.

Often the containers used will have no drainage holes and it will therefore be necessary to install a layer of drainage material on the floor of the vessel. This provides essential air spaces in which water will be rapidly sucked when the plants are watered. One of the best drainage layers and one of the simplest to provide is made of small nuggets of charcoal. At one time broken flower pot crocks were used but clay pots are becoming rarer and rarer and it is best not to depend on having enough broken pieces to provide the drainage material. Stones and shingle may be used as well but they tend to make the bowl very heavy.

The first rule for a successful dish garden is to provide good soil. Although the plants will retain their pot soil or root balls, more soil will be needed to pack round them. Do not use soil that has been dug up from the garden or countryside as this is likely to contain harmful pests and fungi. Buy a bag of potting compost for the purpose. Unless you are making many dish gardens, buy a small amount of potting compost as it tends to deteriorate during storage.

Before deciding which container you are going to use, examine your plants. The depth at which they should be planted is determined by their crowns, the part of the plant at the junction of root and top. The crowns should never be further above or below the new soil level than it was originally.

The soil surface need not be level in the finished arrangement, indeed it is often better if this is not the case. Raise it in the centre or on one of the sides. A raised soil area will give the plant a greater depth for its roots. If you are using plants from varying sized pots, you can plant those from the larger pots in the raised area. Plants which like to be well-drained such as sansevierias, peperomias, succulents and bromeliads should be planted in this raised area.

Having decided which plants you intend to plant together, water them and let them drain well before you begin. Knock them from their pots one at a time if you are using this method of making a dish garden, making sure that their roots are exposed to the air only as long as is necessary. It is a good idea to have decided on the general arrangement of the plants in the container before removing the plants from their pots so as not to prolong this exposure to air.

Spread a layer of soil over the drainage layer. Do not make this too deep or you may have difficulty in fitting the plants into the container. As you arrange the roots of each plant on the soil, determine whether and where the soil needs to be raised. Disturb the roots as little as possible.

Most of the plants should be arranged to stand upright but if you want some of them to trail over the edge of the container, or to lean from the centre, tilt them and put some soil under them to wedge in position. Press this down firmly so that the plant is solidly anchored. Guard against panning the surface, however, that is, making it so hard that water cannot pass through it. If water flows

Below left : Another arrangement of foliage plants including a brightly-coloured croton, Begonia Rex, Spider plant, tradescantia and varieties of ivy and fern is given an accent of colour by a pretty primrose in flower.

Below right : This elegant dish garden includes a central white poinsettia around which are planted sansevieria, rhoicissus and geraniums. Two large and cascading ivy plants add grace and balance to the composition.

Right : This ensemble of house plants includes a lovely dish garden of ivies, tradescantia and Spider plant. A rubber plant, philodendron, and beautifully cascading Spider plant complete the selection.

off, the surface is too hard. Make sure you have left enough room for watering. The soil level should be at least half an inch below the rim of the container, even if it rises in the centre.

When all the plants are in position, water the arrangement carefully, preferably by spraying the leaves and the surface of the soil. It is important not to soak the soil. Stand the arrangement in the desired position out of direct sunlight.

If after some time the plants have done well and have spread over

the surface of the soil, you may find the arrangement difficult to water. In this case it is possible to lower the whole container into a sink or some other large vessel filled with water. Hold it until the bubbles stop rising to the surface and then allow the surplus water to drain away. Cacti often need this method of watering, but remember not to do this more than once a month in winter.

It is not a good idea to mix cacti with other kinds of house plants. Fortunately, they make charming arrangements when grown together and there is sufficient variety in shape and colour to make interesting contrasts. Some succulents go well with them, especially those with blooms on their leaves or those which flower well, such as rocheas and crassulas. Sansevierias can be grown in the same arrangement as cacti.

Some succulents can be mixed with the majority of the other house plants you are likely to use in dish gardens. Try to achieve an interesting balance of types of plant in your arrangement, with succulents and other house plants complementing each other.

Most plant groupings are made more varied and dramatic by having a plant or two hanging over the edge of the container. Many types of house plant and some succulents will do well in this role. Plant rosettes or distinctive broad-leaved plants in the centre of the arrangement such as the beautifully marked *Begonia rex* varieties, calthea, maranta, pilea and some bromeliads. For height and grace, there are palms, sansevieria, fatsia, elegantissima, ivies trained to grow vertically, dracaenas especially the attractive *Dracaena marginata* and the green and white *D. sanderiana*. The combinations are endless as are the possibilities for creating a delightful arrangement of plants. The final choice must be a matter of personal taste, but a few typical groupings are:

Pot grown eranthus or winter aconites, double tulips and yellow hyacinths arranged with chlorophytum in a shallow trug basket makes an attractive dish garden. Driftwood and moss hide and support the bulbs which are planted in potting compost.

Large-size arrangements:

1

Chamaedora elegans 'Bella'	*Peperomia obtusifolia* 'Variegata'
Dracaena sanderi	*Sansevieria trifasciata* 'Hahnii'
D. sanderi 'Borenquensis'	*Scindapsus aurea*
Hedera helix 'Scutifolia'	*Syngonium podophyllum*

2

Aphelandra squarrosa	*Hedera canariensis* 'Variegata'
Dracaena sanderi	*Peperomia argyreia*
Ficus benjamina	*P. hederifolia*
Fittonia verschaffeltii	

Medium-sized arrangements:

1

Asplenium nidus avis	*Peperomia caperata*
Dracaena deremensis 'Warnecki'	Poinsettia
Grevillea robusta	

2

| *Calathea ornata* | *Hedera helix* 'Glacier' |
| *Ficus elastica* 'Decora' | *Neoregelia carolinae* 'Tricolor' |

Small-size arrangements (*suitable for a pedestal vase*):

1

| *Hedera helix* 'Chicago' | Saintpaulia |

2

| *Chlorophytum capense* 'Variegatum' | *Begonia rex* |
| | *Peperomia rotundifolia* |

Left : A grouping of plants can be most effective when it includes foliage of different textures, colours and shapes. Here the vivid scarlet of the poinsettia's leaf-like flowers contrasts with the variegated shiny foliage of the Peperomia glabella 'variegata' *and the fluted, heart-shaped leaves of* Peperomia hederifolia. *Further variety is introduced by the striated leaves of the Zebra Plant or* Aphelandra Squarrosa 'Daniae' *and the smooth leaves of the* Ficus benjamina *and* Hedera canariensis.

Below : Here a wonderful variety of foliage is brought together in a plant arrangement. At the centre is a Croton or Codiaeum *and behind it are* Sansevieria, Pittosporum undulatum *and* Hedera canariensis. Tradescantia *and* Vriesia *grow in the front with* Hypocyrta glabra *on the left and* Aphelandra *on the right.*

Some people prefer to grow their house plants in miniature land-scapes complete with diminutive garden features such as paths, pools made of mirror, lawns of mossy plants, bridges and so on. The detail which can be achieved in gardens of this sort is quite staggering, but care must be taken to select plants which will not outgrow the tiny surroundings. Constructing such a Lilliputian garden is a source of delight and is both fascinating, challenging and instructive.

The procedure for planting a miniature garden is the same as for a dish garden although a container which is more like a trough or tray is more suitable to this purpose. Once a layer of soil has been spread over the drainage layer, place one or two rocks so that they are partially submerged and then landscape the surface soil so that it undulates gently.

One or two dwarf conifers or other low growing house plants can then be put in position and the rest of the tiny garden created around them. Alternatively, a small garden of this sort may be made entirely of cacti – creating a desert garden. For this, a sandy soil and plenty of drainage material in the bottom of the container are necessary.

An even more unusual miniature garden can be made by planting a tiny rock garden. When planted in a container of simulated stone made of fibre-glass, the garden becomes as beautiful as its outdoor counterpart. To make it even more realistic in appearance, the container can be painted with stone-coloured emulsion paint.

The container should be filled with good potting soil, with small pieces of rock placed here and there and with the surface of the soil landscaped to make slight valleys and hills.

By treating plants as though they were flowers you can make beautiful and lasting decorations. Here an old ironstone tureen holds a cyclamen, the blooms of which bring out the colour of the tureen. A Begonia masoniana *and a* Plectranthus oertendahlii *with purple-backed leaves cascading over the rim complete the arrangement.*

Most kinds of cacti and succulents will grow well and last for years in a shallow dish providing they are fairly slow growing. In this arrangement, a juniper is added as a contrast to texture but will be transplanted when it outgrows the dish.

There are rock plants which will grow well in this environment such as *Aethionema* 'Warley Rose', *Androsace lauginosa*, *Campanula arvatica* and *C. pulla*, *Erinus alpinus* and *Silene acaulis*. If you want to include a miniature tree, the dwarf willow, *Salix boydii* is suitable. The dwarf conifers are also excellent for this purpose as are some types of bonsai trees and shrubs. Miniature roses such as 'Miss Muffit', which grows to a height of five inches, dwarf geraniums and some of the small bulbs such as *Narcissus minimus*, crocuses and snowdrops will also do well, in a miniature rock garden.

Below : This attractive dish garden includes Aralia elegantissima, Tradescantia 'Silver Queen', Begonia rex, a Croton, Philodendron scandens, Aglaonema 'Silver Queen' *and Hedera helix 'Heisse'. The differences in shapes and textures of the foliage make this a very pleasing arrangement.*

Right : Here is another well-planned example of a dish garden using only foliage house plants. The shiny leaves of the philodendrons and the variegated leaves of peperomia are contrasted with the delicate palm fronds.

142

Bottle Gardens

Left : Ingredients for a puddle pot are simply gravel, water and a lump of charcoal to keep the water sweet. An attractive container and a selection of house plant cuttings completes the requirements. The cuttings are arranged as in a vase, with an interesting focal point in the centre, here a coleus shoot, and trailing plants hanging over the rim.

Nearly a hundred years ago, Dr Nathaniel Ward found that ferns could be grown in tightly sealed glass containers without watering or attention for several years. The moisture which evaporated from the leaves as a result of transpiration condensed on the glass and ran down into the soil watering the plant. The oxygen and carbon dioxide needed by the plants were produced by respiration and photosynthesis. These 'Wardian Cases' in which ferns, mosses and foliage plants were grown have gone out of fashion, but have been replaced by bottle gardens which work on the same principles.

The conditions inside a sealed glass container will suit small, moisture- and shade-loving plants. Plants grown in this way are protected from draughts, dry atmosphere, fumes, pests and diseases.

Below : A bottle garden planted in an old-fashioned carboy includes several varieties of Peperomia. Pieces of bark and rocks are added to give interest to the 'terrain' in the bottle and to give the plants something to lean on if necessary.

Bottle gardens, or jungle jars as they are sometimes called, are extremely decorative and appealing. Apart from this, they play the useful role of making it possible to grow many plants which would not do as well outside the glass walls. You can therefore add to your repetoire of house plants by starting a bottle garden. Some of the more choosy plants you will be able to grow are species of selaginella which are mossy, fernlike and carpeting, *Nertera depressa,* another carpeting plant with tiny leaves and small orange berries, many kinds of tender ferns such as the wiry-stemmed maidenhairs, miniature tender palms, crotons, fittonia, calathea, maranta, peperomia, pellaia, pilea and pellionia.

Some of these plants make good ordinary house plants under certain conditions, but the additional factor which makes them suited to a bottle garden is that they grow slowly. They also provide colour and a contrast of textures. It is of course possible to fill a bottle with only one type of plant such as a colony of bromeliads or ferns, but the more attractive bottle gardens are made of a variety of plants.

Do not be misled into thinking that if a plant is small and has small leaves, that it will be suited for this type of environment. *Helxine soleirolii,* which is commonly known as Mind Your Own Business or Baby's Tears, has tiny leaves but if planted in a bottle it would soon take over the whole area. The same applies to the creeping ficus, to tradescantia and to zebrina. Of course you can always remove a plant from the bottle if it grows too fast and this will eventually be necessary with most types of plant that you are likely to use, but it is a good idea to put off this disruption for a while until the garden is established.

Bottle gardens have become so popular that today special glass containers are manufactured just for this purpose. Of course any large bottle with a wide enough neck is suitable provided that it is made of light-coloured glass so that the occupants receive the maximum amount of light. The old-fashioned glass carboys used for chemicals are usable for bottle gardens, but they have the disadvantage of having a very narrow neck. They have also become very expensive to buy.

An easier type of container to fill is a glass terrarium consisting of a ten to twelve inch diameter bowl fitted with an air-tight lid. A satisfactory terrarium can be made using a goldfish bowl or a

Above left : Before planting a bottle garden make sure that the inside of the glass is clean, and strew a few nuggets of charcoal on the floor of the container before adding sand for drainage. Slope the soil slightly and put the lowest plant in first near the front. Cover the roots of the first plant and then put the next one in position. Be sure to secure the roots of each plant and to firm the soil around it.

Above right : The small Cryptanthus has been tied to a mossy branch before being lowered into the bottle. The Selaginella and tiny fern carpets the soil while the shrubby variegated Euonymus and Carex rush provide contrast of shape and colour. Selaginella has small, scale-like leaves like a tiny fern and the species that are low growing and creeping are ideally suited to the cool humidity of a bottle garden.

disused battery jar or even an outsize brandy balloon type glass. The choice of the container is a matter of personal taste and of manual dexterity: the narrower the mouth of the bottle, the more difficult it is to plant.

The first step in planting a bottle garden is to group the plants as you plan to place them in the jar. It is attractive to slope the soil in the bottle, so keep this in mind when arranging the plants. Some tools will be necessary to plant bottles with narrow necks. Most of these can be improvized using two-foot bamboo canes as handles to the various implements needed. A substitute trowel can be made by cutting off and then straightening the handle of an old teaspoon. The handle is then stuck in the hollow centre of a bamboo cane and held in place with adhesive. In the same way, an old table fork can become a useful rake. Another valuable tool is a rammer made of an empty cotton reel with a bamboo cane rammed in the centre and held with adhesive.

Tools for the maintenance of the bottle garden consist of a long-handled pruning knife which can be constructed by mounting a razor blade in the split end of a bamboo cane and fixing with tape. A pair of long-handled tongs are useful for removing the cuttings

A large brandy-glass type container makes an attractive bottle garden and is easy to fill. Almost any deep glass will serve the same purpose even if the glass is slightly colour tinted. This bottle contains Selaginella, fern, Begonia rex *and* Carex.

and dead leaves from the plants. This can be fashioned from a pair of light kitchen tongs attached to bamboo handles. If this is too difficult, bamboo canes used like chopsticks can be used to remove such debris.

After the chosen glass container has been carefully washed a drainage layer is installed. If an old-fashioned carboy is used for the garden, be sure to wash it with detergent to remove any traces of acid from the glass. Charcoal is a sensible material to use for drainage as it can be poured into the bottle with no fear of breaking the glass. If you use pebbles, stones or crocks, cushion the bottom of the bottle with a little peat to prevent any damage to the glass when the stones are put in.

Make a funnel or cylindrical chute of strong paper or cardboard and insert this in the neck of the bottle. This is an easy way of pouring the soil into the bottle getting a minimum of particles on the sides of the bottle. This process is not necessary if you are using a container with a wider neck so that you can spread the layers with your hand. Soil composts should not be too rich or the plants will grow too fast. The amount of soil you use will of course depend on the size of the container; you should be able to see more glass and plants than soil but it is the depth of the plant's roots which should determine the amount of soil you use.

It is important that the soil be in the right moisture condition before it is put into the bottle. Calculate the amount of soil you will need and take about one third of the amount and spread it out on newspaper to dry. Spray the rest until it is just moist so that when you squeeze a handful gently it clings together. The dampened compost should be put into the bottle first with the dry compost spread over to seal in the moisture. Lightly consolidate the soil with the rammer, sloping the soil if desired.

As with dish gardens, water the plants and allow them to drain before knocking them out of their pots. If the opening of the bottle is very narrow, it may be necessary to shake some loose soil from around the roots so that the plant can be slipped in easily. The leafy part of the plant presents no problem because this naturally contracts as it is pushed roots first through the opening. To be sure of this, hold the plant gently by the tips of its leaves, or if it is tall gather its branches or leaves up near the centre stem so that the plant is made slim and compact.

Make a hole in the compost with a trowel and drop the first plant into position manoeuvering it with the improvised tongs or chopsticks. Start planting near the glass walls so that the following plants do not fall on those already planted, but do not squash the plants against the sides of the bottle. The plants can be held by the tongs or placed on a loop made in the end of a piece of wire and then lowered on to the soil in the bottle. If this is done with care, the plants will not get as much soil on their leaves as if they are simply dropped through the neck of the bottle.

Cover the roots of the first plant and press the soil down firmly with the rammer. Be sure that the plants are set firmly in the soil otherwise they will not be able to absorb nourishment and they may sicken and die. Continue planting in this way until all the plants are in position. A few stones or pieces of mossy bark can be placed among the plants to vary the appearance of the arrangement.

Inevitably some soil particles will have clung to the inside walls of the jar. Do not spray these off with water as it will make the soil too moist. A feather fixed to a bamboo cane or wire can be used to brush the inside of the glass. If the plants' leaves have soil on them, a fine paint brush tied to a cane can be used to clean them.

After the top of the bottle is closed, it will steam up but this will soon clear away. If this does not happen, you can re-open the bottle for a day or two placing it in a well-lit position but avoiding direct sunlight which could cause algae to grow inside the glass.

If the soil is properly moist, the plants should settle in and you should not need to water for some weeks. If the balance is right, you should see a little condensation or dew on the interior every morning. If this seems excessive, there is too much moisture in the soil and it would be wise to remove some to prevent it from running back into the soil. A tissue or piece of sponge tied to the end of a wire is ideal for absorbing this excess moisture. When you see no condensation on the glass, this is an indication that it is time to water. To do this, gently spray the interior glass. This will have the effect of cleaning at the same time. Do not feed the soil or the plants will grow too well.

This attractive glass jar is especially suited for a bottle garden as it has a wide neck making it easy to install the plants and a tight fitting lid. This garden is planted with varieties of Peperomia.

Bonsai

Left : Pyracantha, commonly called Fire-thorn, is an excellent evergreen subject for the art of bonsai. Grow into an upright bushy shape as here, or train into contorted shapes. The berries which turn bright scarlet when ripe and its broad, shiny leaves make it a festive looking plant.

One very pleasing and decorative way of growing plants indoors is to cultivate miniature trees and shrubs. They are all fascinating and can give people who are interested in gardening but have no or little garden a very absorbing hobby.

The dwarf trees and shrubs that are grown indoors fall into two categories. These are first the naturally diminutive examples and second, the artificially dwarfed ones or 'bonsai'.

Most miniature trees, whether natural or bonsai, grow best in shallow containers, not only because such a condition is much nearer to that of their habitats, but also because they look more artistic when planted in this way. Good drainage must be assured with ample drainage holes in their pots. If it is planned to plant the dwarfs in ornamental containers which have no drain holes, a good layer of ballast or crocks should be put at the bottom. The addition of a few lumps of charcoal is also an advantage as it helps to minimize sourness.

A good, although not too rich, soil is the best in which to plant the natural dwarfs. Bonsai, however, require an even poorer soil if they are to retain their diminutive stature. They grow better in a

Below : This type of maple, Acer Seigen, with its beautifully coloured foliage makes a dramatic bonsai tree. Although the plant is deciduous, it can be dwarfed into a shape which is interesting and decorative even when the leaves have fallen.

mixture of two parts commercial potting compost and one part coarse sand. They require regular watering, but no feeding because this encourages unwanted growth.

The most fruitful source of natural miniature trees and shrubs is the dwarf conifers. There are some fascinating, shapely, colourful species and varieties among them. Those classified as real pygmies prove particularly delightful for indoor decoration. Anybody interested is advised to pay a visit to a specialist nurseryman in order to make his own selection. A few good choices are white variegated, columnar *Chamaecyparis lawsoniana* 'Ellwood's White'; *C. pisifera* 'Nana', which is a tight, low bun of dark green foliage; *C. pisifera* 'Nana Aureo variegata', which has a superb golden sheen; *C. pisifera* 'Plumosa Compressa' which is a perfect gem for a pot; *Cryptomeria japonica* 'Bandai-sugi' which has dense moss-like foliage; grey-leaved, columnar *Juniperus communis* 'Compressa'; the globose, blue-foliaged *Picea mariana* 'Nana'; the dwarf yew, *Taxus baccata* 'Nutans'; *Thuja occidentalis* 'Hetz Midget' which is one of the smallest of all conifers; and *T. orientalis* 'Mini-

Below : This bonsai maple is quite old as can be seen from the thickness of its trunk. It has been effectively stunted so that the bonsai maintains the proportions of the full-grown tree. When the maple loses its leaves, the plant is still a dramatic-looking plant.

Top right : Another type of maple, Acer palmatum or Japanese maple, makes a lovely miniature tree. Its crimson leaves and graceful shape can be used to best advantage when the tree's growth is stunted. Here, a lush layer of moss covers the soil in which the tree is planted adding a contrast of colour and texture.

Below right : This bonsai pine has been trained to grow almost horizontally to give an effective windswept look to the composition.

ma', which is exceptionally neat, slow-growing and globose in shape.

As for shrubs, the purple *Acer palmatum* 'Dissectum purpureum' and its green counterpart *A. palmatum* 'Dissectum viridis' have been found to be elegant small trees, lasting for many years. Miniature roses, of which there are many varieties, have also been successful. Other attractive dwarf plants that can be seen at leading nurseries are: very dwarf *Cotoneaster dammeri*, evergreen *Daphne collina*, with deep bluish-green leaves and soft purple flowers, evergreen *Pernettya tasmanica*, which only grows two inches tall and has red berries, and *Santolina chamaecyparissus* 'Nana', which has the most distinctive, white, frosted foliage.

Artificially Dwarfed Trees and Shrubs or 'Bonsai'

The bonsai art, which has been practised in Japan and China for many centuries, is well established in the United States and is becoming steadily increasingly popular in Great Britain. If planning to use miniature trees for interior decoration, it is possible to buy specimens from florists and specialist nurserymen, and to plant them in specially chosen containers. Some of the larger and very old ones are very expensive. Dwarfing trees and shrubs can be a most absorbing hobby for both young and old, not only because it is a form of horticultural and artistic interest, but because if it is practised faithfully, it involves the study of the habits of various trees. It is indeed a vast subject and can only be briefly touched upon in this book.

Quite a number of both native and exotic trees and shrubs are responsive to this treatment. In fact, after some experience has been gained, it is worthwhile trying out any particular favourite. As a preliminary, it might be mentioned that generally plants with small leaves and flowers give dwarfs of good proportion and thus have a correct appearance. An exception to this is flowers growing in racemes, like those of wistaria and laburnum which are always most attractive. Another factor to be considered is that large flowers are not reduced in size.

Centrally-heated, modern rooms with plenty of light make it possible to grow half-hardy dwarf plants such as oleanders and olives indoors in a sunny window. All bonsai must, however, be kept out of draughts and away from intense heat. Spraying with

Above left : A bonsai Hornbeam in winter is a dramatic looking plant even without its leaves. This tree has been trained to grow in a twisted shape which is even more effective when the branches are bare.

Above right : This charming Pyracantha has been trained to grow in an intriguing shape. Such manipulation is an integral part of the bonsai art and gives the plant a dramatic shape as here or the appearance of age. It is achieved by mechanical means such as winding wire around branches and trunks to bend them into the desired shapes, weighing branches down and holding limbs and trunks in place with pegs driven into the soil.

Right : This bonsai chestnut has been pruned into a pleasing shape. It has been allowed to grow upright so that it is the same shape and proportions as a full-size tree. If bonsai chestnuts flower the effect is quite beautiful.

water at room temperature once a week and sponging the leaves occasionally to remove dust is also appreciated. The hardy dwarfs should be put outside in warm rain as often as possible.

The Dwarfing Process
To begin the process, trees and shrubs are started from cuttings or seeds or seedlings found in the garden by planting them in a shallow pan in potting or seed compost. The seeds should be soaked in water for twenty-four hours. The larger ones, such as acorns and beech nuts, should be placed about half an inch down, but smaller seeds less deeply. The pan should be well watered before planting and kept continuously moist. When the cuttings are rooted and the seedlings are two inches high, the dwarfing processes are started. This process is spread over two or three years depending on how slowly the plant grows. The little plants are transplanted to individual containers, using a commercial potting compost. These can be clay or plastic pots but must have ample drainage holes. During

This bonsai evergreen has taken on a very effective contorted shape which makes it look very much like a tree growing in harsh conditions and stunted naturally.

the next two years, the young plants are periodically removed and all the roots growing outside the ball are cut back. Another method is to plant them in small plastic pots like those used for cream or yoghurt. The bottoms and sides of the containers are punched with holes and as soon as the roots protrude, they are cut off. Some growers prefer, as a third alternative, to plant out in the skin of half an orange or grapefruit, which is soft enough to allow the roots to pass through, and then be clipped off.

This process of root pruning continues during the plant's second year, during which time steps are also taken to shape the plant. This is done by pinching out the growing tip with the finger and thumb to encourage it to grow bushy. After this, it is shaped by shortening the shoots one after another and removing completely any undesirable ones. In order to minimize shock, root and shoot pruning should not be carried out simultaneously. Shoot pruning should be aimed at giving a natural outline to the dwarf, similar to that which the large tree would take up on maturity. This process, which must be spread over a continuous period, is best done in spring and summer when growth is at its greatest.

Sometimes it is desired to follow the Japanese example by giving the miniature the appearance of premature old age or perhaps grotesqueness. This is done by mechanical means, such as curling wire around the branches and trunk, so bending the tree to shape, fixing weights to branches to bear them down and twisting the trunk and limbs by tying them to pegs firmly inserted in the soil.

At the beginning of the third year of root pruning, the bonsai should be transferred to their permanent quarters in poor soil, composed of two parts potting compost and one part coarse sand. During this year the plants should be pinched back from time to time to regulate their appearance.

Among the plants readily dwarfed artificially are the conifers, abies (firs), monkey-puzzle tree, chamaecyparis, cedars, gingkos, hemlock spruce, junipers, larch, pines, spruce and yews; the suitable evergreen and deciduous trees and shrubs include acacia (including mimosa), beech, birch, buddleia, colutea, crab apples, deutzia, dogwoods (cornus), eucalyptus, hawthorns, holly, horse chestnut, ivies, jacaranda, laburnum, lilac, maples, oleander, olive, philadelphus (mock orange), poplar, prunus (viz. flowering almonds, apricots, cherries, peaches and plums), pyrus, pyracantha, snowberry tree, tamarix, walnut, willows, winter sweet and wistaria.

Hanging Baskets & Window Boxes

Hanging baskets and window boxes are becoming increasingly popular ways of displaying plants indoors and out. Many trailing foliage plants and some of the flowering varieties look lovely when hung in a basket or stood in a window box. Many plants respond well to this handling especially if they are placed in or near a window. Hanging plants provide a pretty screen in a room or an attractive surround for a window. A window hung with plants can obscure an unpleasant view and bring freshness and life to a dreary room. Or plants in hanging baskets can be hung outdoors on balconies and porches. Window boxes can be used outside on window ledges or on inside window-sills equally well.

Outdoor hanging baskets are usually used for summer flowering plants. They can be made most attractive with a few upright plants combined with one or two trailers. Fuchsias will bloom in a basket all through the summer, as will geraniums and begonias, particularly the varieties of *Begonia pendula*. Ivy-leaved geraniums trailing in a basket with several upright geraniums make an effective display. Lobelias, both the dwarf and trailing type and similar types of nasturtiums do well in hanging baskets.

Outdoor baskets of this sort are often made of plastic-covered wire and should be lined with sphagnum moss before being filled with potting soil. Alternatively, they may be lined with green or black plastic and then filled with soil. Holes should then be punched in the plastic to allow for drainage. Other outdoor baskets are made of plastic with a built-in saucer at the bottom to catch any surplus water as it drains out of the basket. This type of basket is simply filled with potting soil.

Of course when hanging plants indoors, it is important that no water drips from the pot. Specially designed plastic pots are made for indoor hanging plants as well or you can take a plant and its saucer and stand it in a basket or fashion a hanging support around it.

Do not hang plants too high in a room or they will tend to be forgotten when it comes to watering and they may be damaged by the warm air which rises to the ceiling. It is also convenient to hang them at a level so that it is not difficult to water them. Hanging plants can be arranged on a pulley system so that they can be lowered when it is time to water them and then hoisted back up into place.

To plant in a hanging pot, simply put a layer of draining material in the bottom of the chosen container, either pebbles or crocks and a few pieces of charcoal and cover with a shallow layer of potting soil. Knock the plants to be planted out of their pots and place them in the hanging basket filling in around them with more potting soil. Do not pack them too tightly and do not plant them too close to the

This basket of plants hangs from a brightly coloured ribbon. The wire basket is filled with moss which is then planted with trailing ivy. Using hanging plants in this way provides a festive accent for an otherwise plain window.

edge of the pot. Leave a half inch at the top of the pot for watering. Alternatively, plant seeds or small cuttings or offsets in a hanging basket. This method is particularly effective with offsets of the Spider Plant, *Chlorophytum capense* 'Variegatum' which flourishes in hanging baskets and develops new plantlets on long stalks which give the plant a frilly effect.

The plants should be watered and fed normally and dead flowers should be removed to encourage profuse flowering.

The Baby Virginia Creeper *Ampelopsis*, with its green and red leaves makes a useful hanging plant. It can tolerate cool conditions and can be propagated by putting cuttings in water. It can be hung outdoors in the summertime. Its variety *A. elegans* has leaves variegated with white, green or pink.

Asparagus sprengeri or Asparagus Fern with its delicate fern-like shoots makes a fairly hardy hanging plant. It has small whitish flowers which are followed by red berries. It should be sprayed often during the summer months. *Campanula* or Bell Flower has one species *C. isophylla* which makes a good hanging plant. Its flowers are lilac or lavender-blue or white. It too can be hung outdoors in the summer months.

Columnea, the Costa Rican Plant is a pretty evergreen trailing shrub with scarlet and yellow flowers. Although not easy to grow,

Above : This hanging basket is designed for use out of doors and would look lovely hung on a balcony or patio. It is filled with moss which retains moisture but thorough watering is still required.

Right : This hanging plant is suspended from decorative chains. The foliage of the mature plants make it a pleasing rounded shape.

*Left : A decorative
wrought iron cage makes
an excellent container
for a hanging plant.
Tradescantia trails from
the bottom of the cage
and ivy climbs up its
sides.*

*Right : This knotted
hanger provides an
extremely attractive way
of hanging a pot plant.
Large wooden beads
incorporated into the
knotting add accents of
colour. This basket
contains several varieties
of trailing ivy.*

the pretty flowers make it well worth the effort to try. There is one species of jasmine called *J. mesnyi* which is suitable for growing in hanging baskets. It has flat yellow flowers and blooms in the winter.

Linaria cymbalaria, the Kenilworth Ivy is a small trailing plant with blue and yellow flowers that looks very pretty in a hanging basket. Varieties include *alba* with white flowers and *maxima* with large flowers and *rosea* with pink flowers. *Nephthytis* with its arrow-shaped leaves likes to hang in a pot as does *Pelargonium*, the ivy-leaved geranium and *Pilea*, the Creeping Charley. *Saxifrage* or Mother of Thousands is commonly used as a hanging plant. It has long, slender, trailing shoots with tiny plantlets here and there all over the plant.

Oplesmenus and *Scirpus* are both grass-like plants in various colours and do well in hanging pots. *S. cernuus* has thread-like drooping stems which are almost leafless.

Senecio or German Ivy with its fleshy, ivy-shaped leaves makes a good hanging plant. It produces flowers which should be pinched out as they are insignificant. *Spironema* with its large leaves and

An attractively-shaped basket with well grown plants both flowering and trailing.

fragrant white flowers and the familiar *Selaginella* are two other successful hanging plants. *Tradescantia* and nasturtiums and *Zebrina* also do well in hanging pots as do many varieties of ivy and philodendron. The prettiest hanging baskets contain several plants and are, in fact, dish gardens and plant arrangements hung. The same ideas for combining plants apply here as for dish gardens.

If you cannot find pots made for hanging plants, or if you want to make your own hangers, this can be fun and creative to do. Plants stood in a basket can be hung from a cord or chain. Or pots can be suspended in a network of chain. One of the easiest ways of making a hanging pot is to knot a pot plant holder in string. This method of knotting called macramé is becoming increasingly popular as a method of decorating borders and making belts, cords and especially making pot plant hangers. These look fresh and summery whether used indoors or out. A string holder can be made to sup-

Designed for indoor use, this plant trough is a useful way of grouping various plants. Here a cineraria, tradescantia, primrose and variegated ivy are planted together.

port a pot of nearly any size and they can be made very simple or extremely ornate depending on your skill at macramé and the type of plant being hung. You do not want the plant hanger to detract too much from the plant itself, so the more ornate knotting projects should be used for simple plants like philodendrons while the more basic projects are used for the more elaborate plants like a mature Spider Plant. You can incorporate pieces of wood or cork or beads in the macramé to make the design more interesting and varied.

Window boxes can be bought at nurseries and large hardware shops. Most manufactured window boxes are made of plastic in fairly neutral colours, usually dark green or brown. It is possible to find terracotta trough-like containers suitable for use on a window ledge, or even containers made of concrete or stone which can be used. It is important that the container used for a window box is not too heavy because once the soil is added, this will mean considerable increase in weight. And it is preferable if the window box can be lifted in and out of the window so that replanting is made easier and so that the plants can be tended from both sides.

Above : This unusual modern plant hanger is a plastic globe with holes in which the plants are put. Here a croton, aralia and Spider plant in the various compartments.

Left : Geraniums in full bloom overflow this lovely window box. Removing the flower heads once they have bloomed will prolong the flowering time of these plants.

It is an advantage therefore if the window box has handles so that it can be carried without too much difficulty. A simple wooden box made of softwood or even pieces of plywood made to fit together in an interlocking joint system are attractive window boxes. If you are making a wooden box, try to design it without nails so that it can be taken apart easily if you want to store it for the winter months. Wooden window boxes should be made so that there is a gap between the bottom of the box and the window ledge so that the wood is not always wet. Wooden window boxes must be treated with several coats of polyurethane or gloss paint to prevent the wood from discolouring and deteriorating. They can be painted bright colours or even stencilled with floral patterns.

No matter what sort of material is used for a window box, it is essential that the box has good drainage. If you are making a window box, drill several large holes in the bottom piece to allow for drainage. Manufactured boxes should have been designed with drainage holes. Before planting, put a generous layer of pebbles or crocks in the bottom of the box adding a few pieces of charcoal to keep it sweet.

Window boxes or troughs can be used effectively on an inside window ledge as well. Used in this way the plants should be kept in individual pots with a large trough underneath to prevent water from dripping out of the window box. Or if the plants are planted directly into a window trough, it will have to be designed with an overflow container to prevent spills. Stood along the edges of windows or along the floor in a room with large windows, troughs of foliage or flowering plants make an attractive frame to the window.

The selection of plants suitable for window boxes will depend on the effect you are trying to achieve. A group of spring bulbs such as daffodils and hyacinths looks especially pretty outside a window in the early spring months. Geraniums are always a favourite as they provide such generous splashes of colour for the whole summer. The trailing varieties look especially pretty in a window box.

It is of course possible to choose plants which will survive in an outdoor window box throughout the year. Unless the winter months are extremely cold, hardy plants such as outdoor varieties of ivy will make a charming window box throughout the year. Small evergreen shrubs can be planted in a window box and left outdoors throughout the year. These can even be decorated with small ornaments at Christmas time to give the window a festive look from outdoors.

Be sure that the plants selected to grow in a window box do not need too much care. As the conditions outdoors are likely to be quite changeable even in the summer, fragile plants are not suited to be grown in this way.

Above : A fully planted window box with, among other things, cinerarias, geraniums and ivies.

Right : Window boxes built onto the front of a balcony adds colour and interest to the facade of a house. Here geraniums in full bloom fill the window boxes.

168

Arranging Plants

House plants add a special dimension to the decoration of any room, If well-placed, they harmonize with and emphasize the colours and textures of any room. A simple, green plant is likely to suit any setting and if it is planted in a green outer pot, it will merge discretely with its surroundings. Using plants in this way makes them a background in a room. Alternatively, they can play a far more active role in the decor and provide the focal point for an interior through their size, colour and arrangement.

Few leafy plants are just one colour. Even those described as 'green' are unlikely to be produced in one plain, definite colour. Such a plant is likely to have many hues of green; light tints in the young shoots which contrast with the darker green of the older leaves. Often parts of the same plant are very different colours with a different shade on either side of the leaves ranging from hues of green to silvers and dramatic purple, or with different coloured stems or veins. Many green leafed plants have beautifully coloured undersides. Cyclamen and saintpaulias are familiar examples. Conversely, highly-coloured or patterned foliage plants, begonias for instance, often have plain undersides. The texture of the leaves also varies greatly from soft, fuzzy, grey leaves to slick and shiny, green leaves. The amazing thing about house plants is that regardless of which plants you choose to place in a room, they can never be said to clash with each other. Different effects can be achieved with certain plants, but this depends just as much on the shape and texture of the plant as it does on the colouration.

All plants look well together because they are linked by a common colour, green, and they therefore make an analogous harmony. Many plants like flowers have natural colour contrasts and harmonies.

The study of colour is fascinating and by taking interest in the colours of plants we can achieve greater value from their decorative roles in our homes. For example the carmine produced by the familiar green rubber plant *Ficus elastica* 'Decora' in certain stages of its growth may suggest the colour scheme for a room in which the plant stands. Some people prefer to find plants which look well in existing rooms and which bring out the colours of the furnishings, while others let the plants in the room take the lead in suggesting the type of surroundings, colours and textures. A particularly striking plant demands that a room be designed around it in much the same way as a dramatic sculpture or painting or piece of furniture.

Even more decorative impact can be made in a room by the arrangement of flowering plants whose blooms complement the mood of the surroundings. Depending on the effect desired, containers, ornaments, pictures and even soft furnishings can be chosen

Houseplants can be used effectively to enliven an otherwise dull corner of a room. Here a display of plants fills an alcove, with the tall stark rubber plant and decorative fig offset by the profusion of small leaves of the other plants.

to harmonize with the colours of the flowers. Just as is true with leaf colours which never seem to clash with each other, the colours of flowers always go together although of course some associations are more exciting than others.

It is important to have an idea of how colours work together in order to create the most effective harmonies. The colours of plants and flowers are those of the rainbow in which there are three primary colours, red, yellow and blue. From these are derived the secondary colours. If you look at a rainbow, you see how these are made. Blue overlaps with yellow to make green, yellow with red to give orange and red with blue to create purple.

These then are the true spectral colours. As you know, in plant life and elsewhere, colours vary considerably. Just consider for example the number of reds. Each primary spectral colour has its naturally opposed secondary colour which is known as its complementary. Thus orange is complementary to blue, green to red and purple to yellow. You can never create discord if you put two complements together. Think how good a green plant looks inside a red pot.

Sometimes spectral complements are too strong for some people's taste when used in plant arrangements. They may prefer to reduce one or both colours to a paler tint to lessen the impact. In some settings, for example, a green plant might look better in a

A selection of foliage plants stood in an unused fireplace do much to brighten an otherwise gloomy area of a room. Here philodendron and ivy in pots soften the fireplace alcove.

Right: This lovely selection of foliage plants with its contrasts of leaf coloration and shape will enhance an otherwise stark interior. The trailing leaves of two types of tradescantia and of the ivy are balanced by the upright leaves of a palm, sansevieria and Spider plant.

172

pink pot than in a scarlet one. Soft apricot flowers might suit a blue room better than bright orange ones and violet blooms may be more pleasing against pale lemon walls than against buttercup yellow. These decisions depend on the effect you wish the flowers and plants to have on the room, whether you wish them to be dominating and noticeable or to complement the settings and provide a backdrop for the furnishings and other decorations.

Dealing with flowers and plants differs from working with fabrics and paints because there is certain to be some other colour or hue present in every plant, usually green or some hue of it. So when we are making harmonies, we have to take this extra colour factor into consideration. Actually this can be very useful, as green makes a wonderful buffer between one vivid colour and another. The green

This plant-filled interior has a feeling of lushness provided by the profusion of houseplants hanging, climbing and standing. The large windows make the room seem more like a conservatory.

Right : This Philodendron bipinnatifidum has lived for five years in a room where it receives no direct light. Its leaves turn toward the main light source so that the plant's 'back' is to the wall.

leaves of flowering plants provide a calming effect to even the most wildly coloured flowers placed next to each other.

If you are uncertain about the colour of the container in which to put any plant, green is always safe as it is sure to harmonize with any plant. Of course the green of the container could be chosen to exactly match some green in the plants or flowers and then this harmony would be even more pleasing. It is of course always safe to use either black or white for containers as they always look right with plants.

So far as arrangements are concerned, not everyone likes to see contrasts, even if these are harmonious. Many people prefer a subtle blending of hues. Monochromatic arrangements are always popular and can be just as effective visually as a diversity of colours.

There are so many varieties in shape, colour and living conditions relating to indoor plants that it is possible to find a plant for every situation in the house or office. The many shapes, sizes and colours of house plants give enormous scope to decorating a room to meet any taste requirements. They enliven and bring great charm to any setting and do much to perfectly finish many decor schemes. They can be most successful accompanied by flowering pot plants to give cheerfulness to any room in the depth of winter. On hot summer days, by contrast, they can bring a freshness and coolness to the feeling of a room.

The large, shiny, rich green leaves of some plants, and the boldness of their design can lessen the fussiness of a small fabric design. Plants suitable for this effect are some of the philodendrons, *Monstera deliciosa* and *Fatsia japonica*. The small-leaved and variegated foliage of other plants can have the opposite effect of softening the starkness of a sparsely decorated room or of unbroken areas of solid colour in walls and furnishings.

The use of house plants should not be overdone so that they take over a room. They can be made to enhance any room, but an excess of plants can make it seem claustrophobic.

If you go out specially to buy a house plant, it is more than likely that you already have chosen a spot for it. If you are given a plant, the situation is altered and you have to find a spot which is suitable for that type of plant. Light and its quantity, warmth and aspect is very important to the placing of plants.

Many of the popular leafy house plants grow naturally in the shade of the jungle forest. They grow in daylight, but in the kind of daylight which is filtered through a ceiling layer of leaves. Surprisingly, this jungle light has much the same degree of intensity as the light inside our homes. This is why plants of this type make such good house plants.

The most popular flowering plants, on the other hand, originated in sunny, open climates and the more flowers a plant has, the more light it needs when it is grown indoors.

These same conditions are required by any plant which has foliage which is other than green. All variegated foliage, that is leaves of two or more colours, needs good light. Direct sunlight can cause more harm than good to these plants.

After learning that house plants need a lot of light, you may think that a window-sill is the natural place for any plant. But even window-sills receive different degrees or amounts of light depending on which aspect they face. Fortunately, north-, south-, east-, or west-facing, we can find plants to suit any window-sill. Simply keep in mind that the sun pouring in in early morning from the east will have nothing like the burning intensity of the sun shining

This lovely pink-flowering hydrangea picks up and accents the colours of the upholstery fabric. Hydrangeas need plenty of water and regular feeding when they are in flower, so always stand the pot in which the hydrangea is planted inside another pot or in a deep saucer so that it can be watered freely and safely. Keep plants away from too much heat so that the bloom will last longer and once it has finished flowering plant it out into the garden.

176

in a south-facing window at midday or one which faces west on a late, hot summer afternoon. North-facing windows tend to be both shady and cool and are ideal for many, indeed most plants as long as the room is kept warm too.

You can actually watch the influence of light on plant growth. If you leave a plant undisturbed in a window it will gradually turn around to face the light. If you want a plant to grow evenly, it is important to turn it a little each day so that eventually all parts receive the same amount of direct light. Or you can make use of this tendency by growing leafy plants on walls that are opposite a window so that the leaves of the plant always face into the room and show their best faces.

Fortunately many plants will grow in this way, for example all the green-leaved climbers and creepers. The greener and tougher the leaf the farther away from the light the plant can be grown.

Very effective live screens can be created using climbing house plants. Such screens can be made permanent or movable and can incorporate both foliage and flowering plants. Climbing plants like philodendrons or ivies can be trained to cover a trellis or room dividing screen thereby providing a very effective decorative touch in a room.

Plant room dividers are useful in homes designed on an open plan where some division of one area from another is desirable without creating separate rooms or cutting off light from one part of the space. A screen of plants could, for example, provide an attractive divider between a dining room and a living room.

The plants used in such room dividers can be chosen so as to create a more or less dense screen of leaves. *Cissus antarctica,* *Philodendron scandens* or *Tetrastigma voinierianum* make excellent

Below : Geraniums and African violets in bloom fill this decorative basket with colour. Houseplants used in this way make delightful centrepiece arrangements for an informal luncheon table.

Right : The shapes of the foliage of these houseplants are echoed in the wallpaper chosen for this dining room setting. Philodendron stand facing the window along with palms and schleffera. The grouping of plants by the window has the effect of bringing the outdoors into the room.

subjects for a denser barrier of foliage.

Most strong climbers such as *Cissus, Rhoicissus,* ivy and some philodendron varieties can be trained to grow up in the corner of two walls and along the top of the wall in one direction or another or even right around the room. To support the plants, you can stand a cane from the container to the ceiling or you can tie one end of a thread to a short cane to which the plant is already attached and pin this thread to the ceiling. Obviously the thread must be strong and it is most effective if it is not conspicuous. Nylon fishing line is ideal for this purpose because it will support even weighty stems.

If you are going to use plants at high levels, remember that warm air currents rise and that plants could suffer as a result. Those with lush growing tips such as philodendrons are more likely to suffer than say, *Rhoicissus.* To prevent these from drying out, spray the growing tips and the rest of the plant if possible with a little water from time to time. Use an atomizer and water at room temperature.

Variegated plants can be grown in the same way or in a hallway or corridor where the opposite wall is not too far from a window. Variegated ivies will roam decoratively, especially the large-leaved *Hedra canariensis. Scindapsus aureus* and its varieties are useful for smaller effects. This pretty little plant looks well, planted at the foot of the large-leaved ivy. If it is mixed with the dark-leaved *Plectranthus* which has purple undersides to its leaves it will provide a nice contrast.

Bromeliads will flourish in this type of growing condition and a grouping of these plants will provide a decorative accent to any interior. You can even construct a bromeliad tree, a tree planted with bromeliads, quite easily and this will be a dramatic way to display the plants. Driftwood is good for this purpose as its grey colour contrasts with the blue-green of much of the bromeliad foliage and it can often be found with complicated and twisting

A small conservatory has been built out into the window behind this kitchen sink, and a profusion of foliage and flowering houseplants including daffodils, poinsettias, cinerarias, ivies, coleus and a fig tree create a lovely view. African violet and other cuttings on the window sill wait to take their place among the full-grown plants.

shapes with natural cavities for planting.

Preparing the tree or driftwood for planting is a fascinating design job. First imagine where the clumps of bromeliads will look best and then look for natural crevices near these spots – knotholes, patches of decay or forks where the tree has branched. These can be enlarged to accommodate the plants with an auger or heavy gouge. A half inch hole should be bored from the bottom of each crevice to provide for drainage.

The bromeliads are 'planted' by wrapping their roots in sphagnum moss and pressing them firmly into the cavity or crevice. The trick is to use small plants which will take hold quickly and grow successfully. It is essential to apply pressure to the moss around the roots to anchor them securely and to establish contact between the roots and the fibre.

After several months, the bromeliads will fasten themselves in place with a system of roots and will begin to produce shoots and offsets which form into massive clumps. Care is about the same for bromeliads in pots although watering might have to be a little more frequent.

Creating a plant window is a sure way of guaranteeing a lovely view. Here window boxes are brought inside and windows are decorated with hanging baskets of trailing foliage plants to create an enviable view in a window with an unfortunate outlook. This use of plants has the effect of making an ordinary room feel like a conservatory.

Plants also look attractive when placed at right angles to a window. Here, according to the size and style of a room, one can place a shelf, a table, a group of plants stood on the floor or a planter or trough. Grouped in this way you can often use one or two plants to shield the rest from intense light. Place those which revel in light on the outside such as a *Euphorbia splendens* or a large cactus and graduate the rest so that those which prefer shade are the farthest from the light.

If you plan to use a trough in or under a window bear a few points in mind before you install it. Remember that the plants will turn to face outwards in time unless you are prepared to turn the trough every day. Choose plants which look attractive with light shining through the leaves like the ornamental begonias. If you plan to grow climbers in the trough these can look attractive trailed around or covering the window if you want to obscure an unsightly view. Climbers do best when the roots are not exposed to light so plant bushy plants around the base of the climbers or stand the container so that light does not reach the base.

But not all of us will want to put plants in a window. In many homes this is not a suitable area. Dark corners and dim hallways can be enlivened if plants could be grown there and many people want to use plants just for the purpose of cheering up the gloomy areas of the house.

If these areas are lit in some way, you will ensure not only that the plants will be seen, but also that they will be happier because they will receive some light. Artificial light left on for four or five hours a day will greatly improve a plant's performance. If you have

African violets in full bloom provide bright bouquets of delicate flowers surrounded by decorative, fuzzy leaves. The purple mauve and pink shades look well in most settings.

Right: Here again, an array of foliage plants in a window creates a lovely screen of leaves. Because plants turn to face the source of light, it is important when using them in this way, to choose plants that look attractive from the back as well as the front. This selection which includes a lacy aralia, varieties of fig and dracaena and ferns, looks equally attractive from either side of the window.

a plant that has shown no signs of growth for months, try putting a lamp near it and watch the new rate of growth. This is why plants in living rooms often do better than plants in hallways where there is likely to be less artificial lighting used.

You can improve the light intensity in a room and at the same time direct a little more light onto a plant by a few simple means. Plants do better where there are light-painted walls than they do against dark backgrounds. A strategically placed mirror will reflect light from a window or from an artificial source onto a plant. And plants look lovely when reflected in the mirror.

One of the kindest things which plants can do is to bring life to a hearth no longer used for a real fire. The fireplace, as long as it is draught-proof is an ideal place to grow plants. Here they can be watered and sprayed without danger to furnishings or walls. And many of the hearth and fireside accessories make attractive containers. Ash pans, scuttles, coal boxes, log baskets and large preserving pans all make excellent and decorative containers for plants once they are lined with plastic or a few layers of cooking foil. If the lighting can be improved, the variety of plants which will grow in a fireplace can be extended. However, even without this there are plenty of plants which will thrive at this distance from window light. Aspidistras, palms, syngoniums, philodendrons, spathiphyllums, bromeliads and sansevierias are some examples.

Use plants to their greatest decorative advantage. If you are just beginning to furnish your home, use them to fill in gaps meanwhile. You can always move them around when you have decided on something more permanent. Let them mask a dreary scene and take attention away from an ugly or shabby corner. Use them to make your rooms look taller, wider, homelier and more welcoming.

Plants in an Office

Growing plants in an office presents slightly more difficult conditions and as a result the types of plant suitable to 'go to work' are more limited. Although most offices do not suffer from the problem of insufficient light, there are other hazards. Excessive heat, hot radiators, dry air, draughts, tobacco smoke and baking sun can play havoc with even the toughest specimens.

Plants do make an office a more pleasant place to work whether they are grouped in displays in the entrance or placed on window-sills or desks in individual offices. The ever-changing moods of plants can soften the harsh decor of modern offices and can mask the austere lines of contemporary office furniture. Flowering plants can provide that necessary bit of colour to make the office a more cheerful place to be.

It can even be argued that the presence of plants can have a good psychological effect on office workers. Certainly those who are gardeners appreciate them and it has been agreed for a long time that green is a restful colour.

Once a choice of plant has been made for the office, the greatest problem is how they are to be tended during hot weekends and holiday periods when the self-appointed and dedicated office plant lover is away. The only sensible solution is for a house plant contractor to look after the plants during these periods or that the plants be taken home if the office is to be empty for a long period.

Varieties of climbing and trailing foliage plants decorate the walls of this sun-porch. The ivy has been trained to climb up a bamboo cane, and other ivies and philodendrons trail from pots either hung or stood on window sills. The plants which have been chosen for this grouping all do well in cooler temperatures.

There are many companies which buy and own plants and which arrange with a contractor to supply the necessary maintainance. When the plants need replacing this is done by the contractor. The difficulty with this sort of arrangement is often that the plants become shabby and neglected and are refreshed only by being replaced with new plants when the contractor makes his rounds.

The following is a listing of plants satisfactory for office life. They are graded according to their suitability. Those in Grade 1 are excellent; those in Grade 2 are very good; and those in Grade 3 are good and satisfactory.

Grade 1

Pandanus veitchii
Sansevieria trifasciata 'Laurentii'

Grade 2

Aechmea fasciata	*Monstera deliciosa*
Ananus bracteatus 'Striata'	*Philodendron bipennifolium*
Billbergia nutans	*P.* 'Burgundy'
B. windii	*P. hastatum*
Chamaedorea elegans	*P. laciniatum*
Chlorophytum elatum	*P. pertusum*
'Variegatum'	*P. scandens*
Dieffenbachias	*P. tuxia*
Dracaena deremensis 'Warnecki'	*Schefflera actinophylla*
D. godseffiana	*Scindapsus aureus*
D. sanderiana	*Spathiphyllum* 'Mauna Loa'
D. marginata	*S. wallisii*
D. volckaerti	*Syngonium podophyllum*
Ficus elastica 'Decora'	*S. podophyllum* 'Emerald Gem'
Maranta 'Tricolor'	*S. vellozianum*

Grade 3

Aechmea fasciata	*Gynura sarmentosa*
Aeschyanthus speciosus	*★Hibiscus rosa-sinensis* 'Cooperi'
Anthurium scherzerianum	*Hoya carnosa*
Aralia (Dizygotheca)	*Kentia forsteriana (Howea)*
elegantissima	*Maranta leuconeura*
Asplenium nidus avis	'Kerchoveana'
Cocos weddelliana	*Neoregelia carolinae*
Cryptanthus	*N. marechali*
Ctenanthe lubbersiana	*Philodendron fenzlii*
Ficus australis	*P. selloum*
F. benjamina	*Platycerium alcicorne*
F. doecheri	*Rhoicissus rhomboidea*
F. pumila	*Saxifraga sarmentosa*
F. schryveriana	*Scindapsus pictus* 'Argyraeus'
Guzmania lingulata 'Minor Flambea'	*Tolmiea menziesii*

★requires good light.

This lovely array of house plants has spilled out onto the porch where it merges with the plants in the garden. Brightly coloured crotons and stately oleanders flank the doorway and a grape vine climbs across the beam around the room. A mass of flowering geraniums, coleus and ivies blend together to make a pleasing arrangement of colours.

Overleaf: This elegant palm, Kentia Forsteriana, *is a slow growing and fairly indestructible plant. Its graceful fronds make an excellent foil for a plain setting.*

INDEX

189

ACKNOWLEDGMENTS

The publishers would like to thank the following individuals and organizations for their kind permission to reproduce the photographs in this book:

A-Z Botanical Collection: 42, 53 above left, 76 right, 166, 169; Bernard Alfieri: 56, 115 below; Pat Brindley: 71, 77, 91, 92 left, 99, 132 left; Connaissance des Arts: (R. Guillemot) 181; Stephen Dalton: 8–9, 35 left, 76 left, 87, 96 right, 126 above right; W. F. Davidson: 46 below, 49, 53 below; Dobies of Chester: 105 below; J. E. Downward; 10, 12, 13 left, 25, 28, 32, 35 right, 36 right, 38 right, 40, 43, 57, 60 right, 61 left, 62 right, 65 left, 67, 68 right, 69 left, 73 left, 74, 75 left, 82 right, 84 left, 88 left, 90, 93 right, 94 left, 95 left, 100, 108 above right, 109 above, 121 left, 122 above right, 124 right, 126 above left, 127, 130, 131 left, 155, 157; Douglas Fisher Productions: 47; Melvin Grey: 135, 156, 163, 170, 172, 182; Peter Hunt: 27, 41, 66 left, 84 right, 102–103; George Hyde: 46 above left, 53 above right, 55, 105 above, 112 below left, 113, 116, 117 above left; Jackson & Perkins: 54, 118–119, 143, 149, 150; Leslie Johns: 21, 44 above, 50, 51, 106, 106–107, 109 below, 137, 139, 141, 144, 146, 147; Marshall Cavendish: (Chris Lewis) 167; Bill McLaughlin: 23, 174, 175, 177, 178, 178–179, 186–187; John Moss: 60 left, 161; N.H.P.A.: (Bernard Alfieri) 13 right, 15, 31, 34, 36 left, 37, 58–59, 64, 65 right, 66 right, 68 left, 70, 78, 80 right, 81, 86, 88 right, 89, 93 left, 98, 121 right, 122 below, 123, 124 left, 125, 126 below right, 151, (G. W. Docwra) 108 below; E. A. Over: 117 below; Popperfoto: 29, 38 left, 82 left, 95 right, 134, 160, 162, 165, (Violet Stevenson) 128; Malcolm Robertson: 164, 168; Wilhelm Schact: 108 above left; Kenneth Scowen: 44–45, 46 above right, 52, 114; Anthea Sieveking: 6–7; John Sims: 69 right, 79 right, 80 left, 92 right, 96 left, 97; Harry Smith Horticultural Photographic Collection: 22, 24, 39, 48, 73 right, 75 right, 83 left, 85, 94 right, 104, 122 above left, 126 below left, 131 right, 133, 138–139, 142, 145, 152, 153 below, 154 left, 173, 180, 184–185, (P. Hunt) 14, 79 left, (S. Orme) 132 right; Spectrum: 111, 112 above, 112 below left, 115 above left, 117 above right, 120, (Tony Boxall) 26, 83 right; Syndication International: 153 above, 158, 188; Agence Top: 183; W. J. Unwin Ltd.: 44 below.

Line drawings by Liza Kirwan.